# VAUXHALL

# VAUXHALL
# INSTRUCTION BOOK

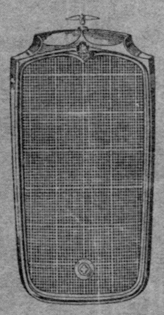

## 12 H.P. AND 14 H.P.
## SIX CYLINDER
## MODELS

### THIRD EDITION

# VAUXHALL

## STUART FERGUS BROATCH

SUTTON PUBLISHING LIMITED

Sutton Publishing Limited
Phoenix Mill · Thrupp · Stroud
Gloucestershire · GL5 2BU

First published 1997

**British Library Cataloguing in Publication Data**
A catalogue record for this book is available from the
British Library.

ISBN 0-7509-1561-7

Typeset in 10/12 Perpetua.
Typesetting and origination by
Sutton Publishing Limited.
Printed in Great Britain by
Ebenezer Baylis, Worcester.

# CONTENTS

# GEARBOX DESIGN—Interesting Comparisons (Illustrated).

## The Motor

Vol. XVII.    No. 422.     TUESDAY, 1st FEBRUARY, 1910.      ONE PENNY

*Registered at the G.P.O. as a Newspaper.*

EDINBURGH
MOTOR
SHOW,
Jan. 28 – Feb. 5, 1910.

Stand
84.

EDINBURGH
MOTOR
SHOW,
Jan. 28 – Feb. 5, 1910.

Stand
84.

Not mere assertions, but
the official records of

### The Scottish Automobile Club

proclaim the fact that no other car has so fine
a list of Successes in Scotland as that of the

## Vauxhall

1907. 1908, and 1909—Every year a veritable
triumph! Ask for a copy of the Scottish
Show Souvenir at

### Stand 84.

Agents for Scotland (excepting Dundee):
MACDONALD & WILKIE,
18, Albany Street, EDINBURGH.

Agents for Dundee and District:
THOS. CUTHBERT & SON.
Ward Road, DUNDEE.

Catalogues by return of post.     Trial runs on request.

**VAUXHALL MOTORS, LTD., 180, GT. PORTLAND ST., LONDON, W.**

STAND
76

# NORTH BRITISH

Edinburgh
Motor
Show.

CLINCHER TYRES.

# INTRODUCTION

The past one hundred and forty years have seen four phases in the history of Vauxhall. First, there were the marine engines and accessories, which were produced from 1857 until just after the First World War. This overlapped with the Edwardian and Vintage motor cars, followed by the mass-produced General Motors Vauxhall car and the Bedford commercial vehicles. Finally there is the German-designed General Motors Vauxhall of the past twenty years. During this period the name Vauxhall has compared very favourably with the best in its field. As with any manufacturer, there have been successes and failures, lean years and profitable times. This book looks at the history of the marine and motor car part of the Vauxhall story, in particular the years between 1857 and 1978.

My own involvement with Vauxhall started at the age of five. By this time I was already 'motorized', as Harry Westlake, the cylinder head designer, had presented me with a splendid tricycle a year earlier. Going to school meant travelling on two buses. Both were Bedfords belonging to the Rover Bus Company. Over the following years I grew to know their drivers very well, men such as Frank Lagadu and my friend Desmond Reid. With a common interest in vehicles, the conversation would often turn to the products of Vauxhall Motors, which were highly thought of by Frank and Des.

Another influence in these early years was Cyril Pratt, who had chauffeured my maternal grandparents for many years. In the late '40s Cyril went into the private hire and taxi business. His fleet was always interesting; he ran at least two Vauxhalls. In the '50s Cyril was hired for longer trips, sometimes going to Hastings for summer holidays and later taking my mother for hospital treatment in Oxfordshire. On those trips to Oxfordshire, while my mother was receiving treatment Cyril and I would talk about cars. He was a great enthusiast of the Vauxhall marque. Thanks to these early influences, I too developed a life-long interest in the products of Vauxhall Motors, both pre- and post-General Motors.

Even when I was Technical Assistant to the Chief Engineer of Saab at the UK headquarters in Wellcroft Road, Slough, I ran a 101 Victor de luxe because it was more reliable than the Saab. Later I joined the excellent Vauxhall Owners' Club, and for the last few years I have been working on the 'ground-up' restoration of a 1934 A-type

The author's maternal grandparents, Percy and Elizabeth Puddephatt, picnicking beside their 1924 Buick 6-50 seven-passenger sedan. Their chauffeur, Cyril Pratt, is sitting in front of another relation's 1920 14/20 HE, with its Bugatti-style radiator. The Buick was a product of General Motors. The Vauxhall R type was fitted with a modified Buick body, as used on the 1925 Standard 6 sedan.

saloon. In the 1980s I got to know Geoffrey King, son of C.E. King, who was Chief Engineer at Luton from 1919 to 1952. As a result of our conversations, the A type is fitted with a 2.3-litre L-type engine, stiffened suspension and, very soon, hydraulic brakes. Geoffrey and I talked about a series of books setting down the history of Vauxhall and the people who made it a success. Sadly he died in July 1989, but not before we had made a number of detailed notes and he had written to his old friend and colleague, Maurice Platt.

Happily, Vauxhall Motors take great interest in the company's history. For a number of years examples of their earlier designs have been collected and restored at their Heritage Centre, which is run by Bernard Ridgeley and Ray Cooper.

In the early 1970s GM took the decision to make Opel the centre for their European car design. As a result of this decision Vauxhalls, from the rear wheel drive Cavalier onward, with the exception of the Viva Magnum and Chevette, became rebadged Opels. On some models there have been variations in trim and minor styling differences.

Over the past twenty-two years the Vauxhall marque has taken an increasingly large share of the UK market. In recent times GM European designs have been considered by many to be superior to those of their rivals. These designs are international in their concept, with designers and engineers from several countries pooling their expertise.

During the past twenty years great changes have taken place at Vauxhall Motors. The famous Bedford truck is no longer manufactured, the Millbrook test track has been sold and today Vauxhall Motors is an assembler of GM's designs. However, the company is now profitable and the products it assembles have never been more popular.

# ORIGINS

The name Vauxhall had its origins in thirteenth-century Plantagenet England. Faulk le Bréauté was a mercenary employed in the service of King John. He was well rewarded for his efforts on behalf of the King and was made Sheriff of Oxford and Hertford, in addition to being granted the Manor of Luton by the grateful monarch. By royal command he married Margaret de Redvers, widow of Baldwin de Redvers, son of the Earl of Devon. Margaret de Redvers was a member of the powerful Fitzgerald family and owned a house at Lambeth. By his marriage to her Faulk le Bréauté acquired her Lambeth house as well as a considerable fortune. When in London le Bréauté and his new bride Margaret stayed at the Lambeth house, and as a result the property became known as Faulk's Hall.

In 1216 King John died and Faulk le Bréauté was exiled to France by his successor Henry III, where he later died in poverty. Meanwhile the house at Lambeth became known as Fawkes Hall and, by 1661, Vauxhall. In that year the New Spring Gardens opened on what had been the site of Faulk le Bréauté's Lambeth estate. In 1667 Samuel Morland built a music and gaming room in the garden. Charles II and Nell Gwyn visited the new attractions and diarist Samuel Pepys refers to the gardens in his writings. In June 1733, seventy-two years after the opening of the gardens, the site was leased to a Jonathan Tyer for a period of twenty years at £250 a year. On the first night under Tyer's management, the gardens were the scene of a celebration which drew some four hundred people, including Frederick, Prince of Wales.

The gardens survived until 1859, by which time they were the oldest pleasure gardens in London. The Tyer family actually ran the site for ninety years. They were followed by a concern known as Bish, Gye and Hughes, but by now the gardens were run at a loss. The character of the area was changing. Lambeth and Vauxhall were becoming industrialized, and with the building of Vauxhall Junction railway station the last remnants of what had been a very pleasant area adjacent to the River Thames were destroyed. Vauxhall Gardens, as they were now known, were sold in 1859 for £20,000.

Two years earlier a young Scottish marine engineer, Alexander Wilson, had set up in business in Wandsworth Road as the Vauxhall Ironworks, taking as the company's badge the Griffin which had originally been Faulk de Bréauté's coat of arms. For many years the Griffin had been above the archway that led into the Gardens. The Vauxhall Iron Works manufactured compound and triple expansion steam engines for tugs, engines for side paddle and stern wheeler ships, such as the popular pleasure steamers of the 1890s, the *Queen Elizabeth* and *Cardinal Wolsey*, which plied between Westminster Bridge and Hampton Court. Wilson had contracts with the Admiralty for the supply of high pressure engines for pinnaces. The company also manufactured donkey engines for boiler feed, the Lightfoot dry air refrigeration plant for cold storage, the 'Excelsior' steam-driven pump, boilers, propellers and shafting.

Up to 150 men were employed at the Vauxhall Iron Works by the 1890s. Wilson was essentially a practical man rather than an organizer. His desk was usually covered with assorted paperwork, old envelopes being used for rough drawings and so on.

In 1892 Wilson's company was incorporated and became a limited liability company. Mr W. Gardner, a marine consulting engineer, became Managing Director. Wilson remained on the board, but in 1894 he left the company he had founded and set up as a consulting engineer in London's Fenchurch Street. In 1897 the company's official name became the Vauxhall Iron Works Company Limited. This followed financial reorganization instituted by J.H. Chambers, who was the Official Receiver. With the change of title the works was generally known in the area as 'The Vauxhall'. In earlier days when Alexander Wilson ran the company it had been referred to as 'Wilson's'.

The 1890s saw the first motor vehicles produced in Britain. One of Wilson's apprentices, Frederick William Hodges, showed great interest in the new form of transport. His interest was shared by Chambers, the Official Receiver. A member of the staff at the time, L.C. Derbyshire, later recalled: 'A motor car was obtained and thoroughly examined and studied, with the idea of eventually producing an independent and improved design. The model examined had its engine at the rear, tube ignition and belt drive. . . .'

Hodges had been experimenting with various types of internal combustion engine. As a result of these experiments a successful single-cylinder engine was built. It featured two opposed pistons and was fitted to Hodges' own boat *Jabberwock*. As a result of several successful runs on the Thames, a decision was made by the company to produce a motor car. According to L.C. Derbyshire a complete car was built but never developed for manufacture, although a number of test runs were completed. After the experimental car Hodges built a five-cylinder radial engine. Although it did run under its own power, problems with cooling and lubrication were not overcome. A single-cylinder engine was then produced. It ran successfully, so a light car was designed to take the new engine.

The design of the first production Vauxhall was well received when announced in the October of 1903. Priced at £136 for the two-seater, the new Vauxhall featured all coil spring suspension, tiller steering, two forward speeds and no reverse. The engine's bore and stroke was 4 in x 4¾ in, and the complete vehicle turned the scales at around 600 lb. Also available was a four-seater model in which the passengers sat ahead of the driver over the engine. The throttle control was on the tiller arm and the horizontal single-cylinder engine had a governor on the exhaust valve which was foot operated.

From the beginning, the Vauxhall motor car competed in motoring events. As early as October 1903 the Wolverhampton & District Automobile Club awarded a certificate to a Mr A.G. Price, who drove his 5 hp Vauxhall (car no. 4) up Hermitage Hill, Wolverhampton, in 5 minutes 46 seconds. There are two survivors of the 1903 5 hp Vauxhall out of total production of some forty cars.

In February 1904 a 6 hp motor car was introduced. For the first time a reverse gear was part of the specification, as were artillery wheels. The overall weight increased by 112 lb, and from September the tiller was replaced by a steering wheel.

Reliability trials were popular with motor vehicle manufacturers at this time, and an early example of the new 6 hp Vauxhall was entered in the Glasgow to London Trial. The 6 hp Vauxhall was the smallest car entered. With Managing Director Percy Kinder and designer/director F.W. Hodges sharing the driving, the new car performed well, losing only 7 points out of 1,000 over the entire route, as the sparking plugs had to be changed. At the time, the magazine *The Autocar* commented on the Vauxhall's excellent performance. At Barnet in Hertfordshire Woodcock Hill was climbed at an average speed of 2 mph, in 1 minute 29 seconds. The overall fuel consumption for the entire run worked out at 38.25 mpg. The car was also entered for the Light Car Trials, but had to retire on the third day of this 600-mile event with a broken con rod.

1904 had seen production rise to seventy-six cars for the year. In November of that year the company introduced a new model, the 3-cylinder 12/14 hp. At £375 the 12/14 was a larger car than previous models. The water-cooled T-head engine was of 2.4 litres capacity with the cylinders separately jacketed, as were the majority of designs at this time. A three-speed gearbox and double chain drive took the power to the rear wheels. For the first time on a Vauxhall half-elliptic leaf springs were used.

With increasing production, the original London site was proving to be too small. The telegraphic address 'Wellhole, London' was rather apt as motor cars had to be lifted from the basement by a hoist. There were also problems at the time with the lease. The original Vauxhall factory employed up to 200 staff in 1904, engaged in the production of the Vauxhall motor car. The site of Vauxhall Walk covered one acre, compared with the quarter acre originally used for marine production. In 1904 negotiations took place for the purchase of a new site at Luton, Bedfordshire. At this time Luton was best known for the manufacture of straw hats. However, the town had recently built its first municipal electricity supply undertaking and with plenty of male labour this was a commercially sound move. The transfer of production to the new 7-acre site 30 miles north of London took place early in 1905. Because of this upheaval, production of Vauxhall cars for the year was down to twenty vehicles.

The same year saw Frederick William Hodges introduce his 7/9 hp car, which was a downrated version of the earlier 12/14 hp car with a reduced engine capacity of 1.3 litres. The design was not a success; many examples suffered from over bodying and production ceased at the end of the year. At the London Motor Show a 1.4 litre 9 hp design was introduced. Again the engine design was based on the original 12/14 model.

In the Isle of Man Tourist Trophy Race of 1905 ex-Vauxhall marine engine apprentice Alfred John Hancock drove a modified 12/14 car fitted with a six-speed overdrive gearbox. Alas, on the second lap a wheel broke when cornering, putting the Vauxhall entry out of the event. A.J. Hancock sustained slight injury to himself. In later years Hancock was to become well known for his racing and record breaking attempts driving Vauxhall works' cars. The other important event of 1905 on the motor car front was the introduction of Vauxhall's first four-cylinder motor car, the 18 hp in November. The engine was of the T-head type and had a cubic capacity of 3.402 litres; 23 bhp was developed at 1800 rpm. The engine featured five main bearings and was a definite improvement on Hodges' earlier designs.

Vauxhall's famous flutes first appeared on the new 18 hp model. This first design featured parallel flutes each side of the bonnet, as opposed to the tapered designs which became familiar to later generations of motorists. Also appearing was the first example of what would become Vauxhall's traditional radiator shape for many years. The story goes that the shape of the radiator was patterned after mouldings on a wardrobe in a director's bedroom! Despite its unusual origin the traditional Vauxhall radiator was undoubtedly one of the most handsome and enduring of British designs.

Vauxhall's nearest neighbours on the new Luton site were the West Hydraulic Engineering Company and a farmhouse, both of which appear in a number of early Vauxhall photographs. Apart from a row of cottages to one side of the house the rest was green fields.

In 1906 the Vauxhall Iron Works amalgamated with the West Hydraulic Engineering Company to form the Vauxhall and West Hydraulic Engineering Company Limited. At the same time the company's head office moved from London to Luton. In the same year a remarkable young man of twenty-three, Laurence H. Pomeroy, joined Vauxhall as an assistant draughtsman. Pomeroy's brilliance as an engineer would result in the marque becoming, within a few years, pre-eminent in its field. Laurence Pomeroy was born in 1883 and before joining Vauxhall had served a premium apprenticeship with the North London Railway at Bow. He also worked for a very short period of a few months with John Thorneycroft & Company Limited of Basingstoke, Hampshire, who had entered the motor car market in 1903 with a 10 hp two-cylinder design and a 20 hp four-cylinder design.

In 1907 Laurence Pomeroy designed his first Vauxhall motor car: the 12/16 hp designed to replace the 18 hp Hodges design. The T-head four-cylinder engine had a reduced capacity of 2.5 litres, five main bearings and a bore and stroke of 92 by 95 mm. Although 900 cc smaller than the 18 hp engine, bhp was increased from 18 at 950 rpm to 23.5 at 1800 rpm. A three-speed gearbox was used with shaft drive. The new design sold at £375. The last of the old 18 hp models were sold in November 1907. Pomeroy's first design was a success, outselling its predecessor and showing that the company was moving in the right direction.

This very practical background in engineering, coupled with Pomeroy's appetite for absorbing technical theory, enabled him to outdistance other contemporary British designers, particularly in terms of engine theory and practice. Pomeroy's bible at this time was a French book on the basics of automobile design, entitled *L'Automobile à l'Essence: Principes des Construction et Calcul* by Heirman. He had failed his 'Matric' because of his lack of knowledge of the French language, but his solution was to purchase French books dealing with subjects in which he was already knowledgeable. Heirman's work stressed the importance of high compression ratios and large valve areas.

During the winter of 1907/8 F.W. Hodges went on vacation to Egypt to escape the cold English winter. Pomeroy was by now Hodges' assistant and while Hodges was away the Royal Automobile Club published its rules for the 1908 2,000-mile International Touring Car Trial. Vauxhall's directors decided to enter this important event. Pomeroy guaranteed an increase in the output of the existing four-cylinder engine from 23 bhp to over 40 bhp. Within a short period of time the engine produced 38 bhp at the then uncommonly high engine speed of 2400 rpm. He raised the compression ratio to the point where the engine pre-ignited if full throttle was used for more than five minutes. With its five-bearing crankshaft and full pressure lubrication for all the bearings, the basis of the classic Pomeroy-designed four-cylinder L-head side valve Vauxhall engine was laid down with this design. The trials car was completed by June of that year. The car's four-speed gearbox was a conversion of the existing three-speed unit; a separate lever was used to select reverse gear and a torque arm controlled the rear axle.

The 20 hp trials car driven by Percy Kidner was very successful in the 2,000 mile event, losing fewer points than any other car and thus becoming the first motor car to cover 2,000 miles without an involuntary stop. This kind of performance brought the name of Vauxhall and Pomeroy's 20 hp design into the full glare of public interest. The great Edwardian Vauxhall had arrived! A slightly modified version of the trials car known as the A type was put into production in the same year, 1908. The engine size was reduced from 3138 cc to 3053 cc as a result of the reduction of the bore and stroke from 91 x 120.65 mm to 90 x 120 mm.

The following year, 1908, the 16 hp B type arrived with a 2315 cc engine coupled to a three-speed gearbox, as opposed to the A type's four-speed unit. A number of different body styles were offered on the B-type chassis including a two-seater 'semi-racer'. The B type was not as successful as the A type. In all, 150 vehicles were sold before production ceased in 1910. The competition success of the A type continued.

A few years earlier in July 1907 the world-famous Brooklands racing track opened on what was part of Hugh Fortescue Lock-King's enormous estate near Weybridge, Surrey. At the time there was a 20 mph limit throughout Britain. Many of the establishment were against the motor car, for various reasons. Such attitudes severely hampered the British motor industry. When opened in July 1907 Brooklands was undoubtedly the finest circuit of its kind in the world. The final part of the RAC 2,000-mile Trial of 1908 was a 200 mile 'speed test' on the new circuit. Percy Kidner led the field. To many this showed that the new Vauxhall was both fast and reliable for its time.

In the August of the following year (1909) a 20 hp A type driven by Rudolph Sells gained three firsts, two seconds and three thirds. These were the company's first racing successes on the track. In the same year the A type had class wins in the Scottish and Irish road trials and scored the highest average speed (15.9 mph) while ascending the Brookland's Test Hill (gradient 1 in 4). The driver was Percy Kidner. Following these and other successes a streamlined torpedo-shaped body was built on a 20 hp chassis, with a view to breaking a number of speed records and class records. The single-seater was called KN after the pepper, and, driven by A.J. Hancock, proved to be very hot stuff! On the car's first outing Hancock achieved a record win at Shelsley Walsh hill climb and later, in December of the same year, the 21 hp class records were broken at Brooklands with a new speed of 88.6 mph for the flying half mile. The distance record was also broken on this occasion, with Hancock driving ten laps at 81.33 mph. By this time the 20 hp engine fitted to KN produced 52.6 bhp. Pomeroy's approach of progressively improving the performance of his 20 hp engine resulted in the company obtaining 'a considerable reputation in both club and open hill climbs'. By 1910 Laurence Pomeroy had managed to extract 60 bhp from the 20 hp engine. On 7 October a streamlined 20 hp motor car was taken to Brooklands with a view to breaking the 100 mph record for the first time with a 20 hp car. It took A.J. Hancock three attempts to achieve the desired result. On 7 October 97.15 mph was reached and on the second attempt on 22 October a speed of 98.1 mph; Hancock and his team came to the conclusion that oil drag in the car's gearbox and rear axle was preventing the car from reaching their goal of 100 mph. In view of the short distance involved it was decided to drain the oils. Hancock then took the car up to 100.8, thus becoming the first man to reach 100 mph with a 20 hp car over the flying half mile. The car used in these three attempts in October was powered by the engine from KN in another 20 hp chassis, with a modified streamlined single-seater body.

In the same year Pomeroy was promoted to Works Manager. Also in 1910, Vauxhall Motors entered the Prince Henry Trial with three 20 hp A-type cars on the standard 9ft 9in wheelbase. The company entered a three-car team. The cars were fitted with high-sided doorless bodies. Although these were not particularly handsome, the new V-fronted radiator was. Short flutes merged into the bonnet, giving a purposeful appearance to the front end of the motor car. The development of the famous flutes during the period up to 1919 was the work of Pomeroy. It is said that he spent considerable time calculating the relationship between the main curve in the centre of the bonnet and the radius of the two flutes.

The event covered 1,200 miles and was instigated by Prince Henry of Austria to be a demanding trial for touring cars. The Vauxhall team was in competition with some of the best cars of the day, competing against teams from Rolls-Royce, Austro-Daimler and Benz, for example. The three Vauxhall cars were fitted with the 60 bhp version of the 20 hp engine, which gave them a top speed of 72 mph. Originally Pomeroy had planned an overhead camshaft engine for the cars entered in this event. The overhead camshaft was designed so that it could be moved endwise. Double the normal number of cams were used for an eight-valve engine so that it was possible, by moving the camshaft endways, to give one valve timing maximum torque at low speeds and another setting for maximum power output at around 2,800 rpm. The engine's undoing was the oversized inclined valves. The gas velocity was very low and the power output was less than the original 1908 side valve engine. The Vauxhall works' entries driven by Kidner, Hancock and Sells acquitted themselves well in the event. Kidner and Hancock incurred no penalties whatsoever, while Sells incurred minor penalties. The Luton-built cars were 100 per cent reliable and although the winner, the Austro-Daimler 22/80 ps of 5.7 litres and 95 bhp, driven by its designer Ferdinand Porsche, gained a lot of publicity for its manufacture and designer, many informed motorists in Britain recognized that the real winner in terms of efficiency and design was the Vauxhall. The company was successful in the same year in repeating their win of the previous year in the O'Gorman Race at Brooklands.

At the same time the production of the 16 hp B type continued. At the Motor Show in November 1909 the company introduced its first six-cylinder model, which was nominally rated at 27 hp. The general design of the chassis followed that of the four-cylinder 16 and 20 hp models. The engine itself again followed the general lines of the four-cylinder models, being of a monoblock type (in which the cylinders are cast in one block). The new model was referred to as the 27 hp B type. During this period many chassis left the Luton works to be bodied by bespoke coach builders in a wide variety of styles.

In 1909 the firm's output was 197 chassis. A year later this had grown to 246, and in another twelve years the yearly output would be over a thousand vehicles. The marine side of the business still produced a wide variety of equipment, which was advertised in a comprehensive catalogue. In 1912 the most powerful marine engine was of 400 ihp.

Men working in rather primitive conditions at the Vauxhall Iron Works, 1890s.

Vauxhall Pleasure Gardens, Lambeth, in their heyday towards the end of the eighteenth century. 'Then oft returning from the green retreats where fair Vauxhallia decks her sylvan seats, where each spruce nymph from City counter free, Sips the frothed syllabub or fragrant tea; while with diced ham, scraped beef and burnt champagne Her prentice lover soothes his amorous pain.' (Rt Hon George Canning)

Another eighteenth-century print showing something of the merriment and rakish pleasures that the gardens became famous for. Thackeray extols the virtues of the Vauxhall Gardens in *Vanity Fair*, though by Thackeray's time they were said to be the haunt of gamblers, thieves and ladies of easy virtue.

A Vauxhall marine engine designed for a paddle steamer. Many such engines were built from 1857 onwards.

A painting showing the Thames river tug *John Mowlem*, which was powered by a Vauxhall marine engine, at work on the Thames in about 1870.

A small assembly line photographed at the original works, Vauxhall Walk, Lambeth, *c.* 1900. The crankcase in the foreground is stamped Vauxhall Ironworks Co. Ltd.

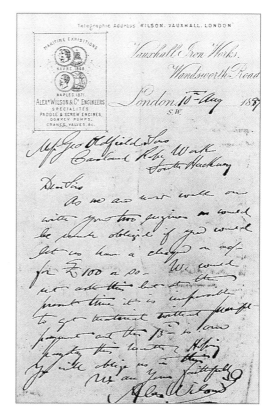

A letter from Alexander Wilson dated 10 August 1889. 'As we are now well on with your two engines, we would be much obliged if you would let us have a cheque on A/C for £1000 or so. We would not ask this but at the present time it is impossible to get material without prompt payment and this 13th is our pay day this month. Hoping you will oblige us in this.'

This is F.W. Hodges' river launch *Jabberwock* in action on the Thames. Hodges is seen at the rear of the vessel. Some time between the years 1896 and 1899, Hodges had designed an opposed piston single-cylinder engine to power *Jabberwock*. The new engine performed well and Hodges was given the firm's backing to design and manufacture an engine for powering a motor car.

The first Vauxhall motor car was the 989 cc 5 hp machine introduced in 1903. The single-cylinder engine was mounted horizontally. The vehicle had two forward speeds, no reverse, foot operated governor on the exhaust valve, throttle control on the tiller steering arm with the power transmitted to the rear wheels by a Brampton roller chain. Top speed was around 25 mph, and was arrested by leather-lined band brakes on the rear wheels. Other points of interest are wire wheels and all coil suspension. The price was £136 for the two seater. Extras were a leather hood for 16 guineas or a buggy-style canopy for 7 guineas. A four-seater model was also built. The first Vauxhall car engine was bored by Harry Pratt. Mr Pratt retired in 1946 and died in 1964 aged ninety-three.

Early Vauxhall motorists pose for the camera, 1904. The venue is Exeter. One of the four-seater 5 hp models of 1903 is shown, as well as three two-seaters of the same vintage.

A 1904 two-seater. The 1904 models had wooden wheels, a reverse gear, 6 hp and 1039 cc. The car sold for £375. Later in the year the tiller was replaced by a steering wheel.

Two examples of the Luton-built three-cylinder car, which featured double chain drive and half elliptic leaf springs. The top photograph shows a restored 7 hp example from the Vauxhall Heritage Centre, and the bottom photograph shows a new 12/14 car near the Luton works.

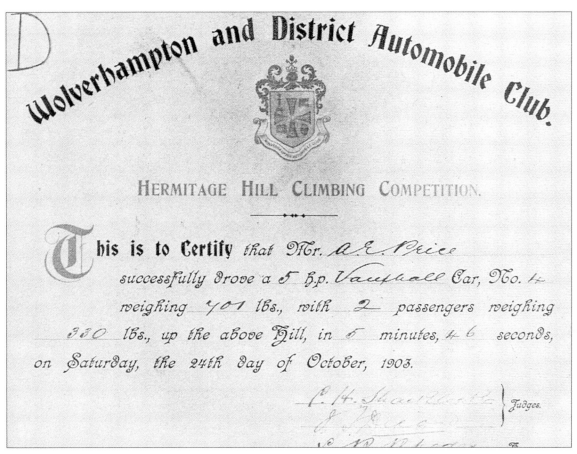

From early days Vauxhall Motors entered sporting events. The first known event was in 1903 when a Mr A.E. Price drove a Vauxhall 5 hp weighing 701 lb with two passengers weighing 330 lb up Hermitage Hill, Wolverhampton in 5 minutes 46 seconds on Saturday 24 October.

A famous photograph showing the first three cars produced at the new Luton factory in 1905.

A motorised hansom cab produced by Vauxhall Motors to a design suggested by the Earl of Ranfurley. The chauffeur steered and controlled the vehicle from the rear!

A close-up of the near side of a three-cylinder 12/14 hp engine of 1906.

The exhaust side of the 20 hp 2138 cc four-cylinder engine designed by twenty-four-year-old Laurence Pomeroy, which was the basis of Vauxhall's entry in the 1908 RAC 2,000-mile International Touring Car Trial, and later powered the A-type car.

The following sequence of photographs illustrates a selection of body styles from the 1906–8 period. This tourer is a 12/14 hp of 1906 or 1907 vintage. Vauxhall's famous flutes appeared one year earlier on the 18 hp.

This landaulette with exposed driving position is a 20 hp model of 1908. Notice the elaborate colour scheme of vertical stripes on the rear half of the body.

This elegant design with covered accommodation for the chauffeur is thought to be a 12/16 hp model of 1908.

Vauxhall Motors' plant of 1905 is the white building in the centre of the photograph. The building to the left is the West Hydraulic Engineering Co., while the larger house to the left of the cottages in the photograph is shown in many early Vauxhall pictures.

The body painting and polishing shop, c. 1908. The coachwork was hand-painted and varnished to a very high standard. The finish was superb but required constant attention from the owner's chauffeur.

The Luton erecting shop, 1911. Nearest the camera is a C type Prince Henry, regarded today as one of the first real sports cars. It had a top speed in excess of 60 mph.

A famous photograph of Laurence Pomeroy at the wheel of a prototype Prince Henry (C type) at Lynmouth, Devon, after prolonged testing.

A selection of 20 hp models spanning the years between 1909 and 1911 are shown in the following sequence of photographs. Tenant's Landaulette shows the style of interior trim used on quality cars of this period. There was still little weather protection for the chauffeur.

Lettridge's standard 20 hp tourer underlines this point.

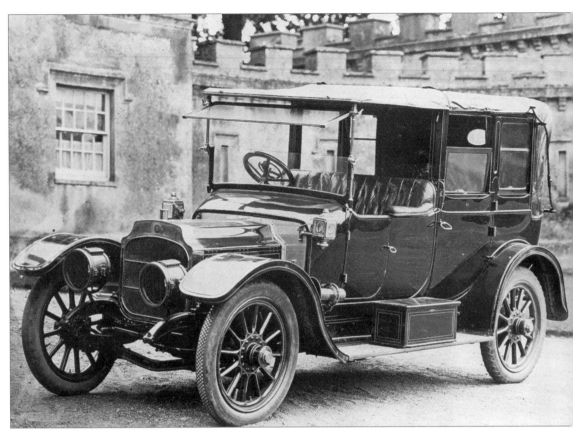

The Sutherland looks if it has seen some use judging by the state of the hood; again the car dates from 1911. Notice the beautiful gloss of the paintwork. The hand-painting and varnishing of high quality cars such as Vauxhalls died out in the late '20s. The R type of 1927 received a spray finish.

The 20 hp had a wheelbase of 10 ft 3 in, which is well illustrated on the Torpedo Touring Car. The customer had a choice of wire or wooden wheels.

Hood design during this period had a very old-fashioned look, as shown on this 20 hp two-seater.

The two seater and the Norfolk show to good effect the high scuttle favoured by Vauxhall Motors around this period.

A six-cylinder B type, first introduced towards the end of 1910. Although in later years Vauxhall were noted for their excellent six-cylinder engines, neither the B type nor the later S type were very successful.

An early two-seater Prince Henry or C type of 1912 vintage with a rather rakish body, which was delivered to the Holingdrake Automobile Co. of Stockport, of which Joseph Higginson was a director. Higginson is regarded as the person responsible for the 30/98.

Vauxhall's works team for the Prince Henry of Prussia Tour. Two cars were entered, driven by Kidner and Hancock. The original caption on the photograph says 'Prince Henry Trophy Cars – Messrs Pomeroy, Kidner, Holton, Hancock and Jack up'.

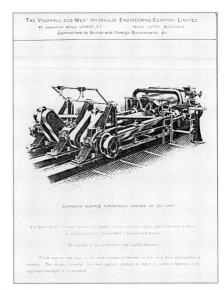

A selection of photographs from the Vauxhall and West Hydraulic Marine Catalogue of 1911. Vauxhall Motors Limited was formed in 1907, and the amount of information available within the present-day company on West Hydraulic is very sparse. There is no mention in the Board Meeting Minutes of anything concerning West Hydraulic other than to record land purchases.

At the beginning of the First World War West Hydraulic was still operating. In November 1916 Vauxhall purchased two acres of land from West Hydraulic and this subsequently allowed Vauxhall to expand its operations and build a laboratory, an apprentice school and a large machine shop. West Hydraulic retained three acres of land at that time which Vauxhall ultimately built on in 1932–4. Looking at some debenture stock of West Hydraulic and the endorsements on the back, this would suggest that the majority of West Hydraulic was wound up in April 1918, because at that time a large amount of money became available to purchase the debentures.

It is logical that the company survived the First World War as it was manufacturing steam engines, which were used in tugs and pinnaces, for the war effort.

West Hydraulic obviously existed in some form from 1918 onwards because it was not until February 1927 that Vauxhall finally purchased the last bit of West Hydraulic land.

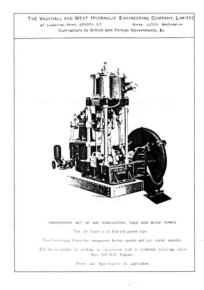

# 1910–1919: A NEW ERA

The production of the Vauxhall motor car at this time involved extensive hand-finishing of components, and was slow and laborious work. Workers would arrive at the factory at 6 am and leave at 5 pm. Apprentices would often go to night school, up to three evenings per week. Firms such as Vauxhall relied heavily on skilled craftsmen. Of these the key man was the 'marker-off', since it was his interpretation of a drawing that the job in hand depended on. Initially the 'marker-off' would select the best average castings or forgings; these were known as 'favoureds'. It was the skill of the marker-off that frequently saved valuable parts from being scrapped. Marking-off consisted of adding centre-punch dots and scribed lines which were used as a guide by the machinist. In the case where more than one individual part needed to be marked-off, a template was made, often using sheet steel. Such templates were made to fine limits and were jealously guarded by the marker-off.

Equal care had to be exercised by the machinist, who would leave a witness line or split dot to prove his own interpretation of the marking. It was then up to the fitter to decide the line from which he could work for his assembly. When lining up crank case bearings for example, prior to hand-scraping, it was necessary for the fitter to select the bearings that needed to be scraped first in order to accept the test bar. The five-bearing crankcase of the 20 hp Vauxhall engine made such a task more difficult when it came to real accuracy. The fitting of the crankshaft to the crankcase was a long operation. If the crankshaft was able to be turned by a lever of less than 2 ft in length the assembly would have to be dismantled, as the fit between the bearings and the shaft would be too slack for running-in.

Complete assemblies were assembled by individual fitters and often stamped, as in the case of engines, with the fitters' initials.

The testing section was where finished engines were run-in, followed by stripping down, final scraping and adjustment. The engine would then be installed in a chassis and at this point the running shed took over. Here the tester would drive the chassis on the road in order that final adjustments could be made.

Vauxhall's directors were obviously delighted with the performance of their entries in the Prince Henry Trial. In the following year of 1911 the company entered the Russian reliability trials, held in the September of that year. Before the Bolshevik revolution, the Vauxhall motor car was popular with the Russian Imperial family and the Russian court. Vauxhall Motors had workshop facilities in St Petersburg run by Mr S. Ovsiannikov, who, in the Vauxhall tradition of that time, was himself an accomplished driver on the racetrack. In addition, Vauxhall Motors published a handsome catalogue especially for the Russian market. A 16 hp car was entered for the Russian event driven by Percy Kidner, Vauxhall's extrovert joint managing director, who had obviously lost none of his enthusiasm for demonstrating the marque's capabilities. The course was from St Petersburg to Sebastapol. Not for the first time Kidner won his class without losing any points in the process.

At this time sales of the 16 hp were slow, which could explain why this model was entered for the Russian trial and also why a successful attempt in a car with a much modified engine was made in the November of that year. This was the time of the long stroke engine and the decision was taken to use a bore of 80 mm with a 200 mm stroke! This resulted in a very tall engine with a cylinder head projecting through the bonnet cowling, which spoiled what was otherwise quite a streamlined body by contemporary standards.

On 4 November the 16 hp Vauxhall covered the flying half mile at 97.7 mph, thus taking away the record from Peugeot, who up to this time had been the leader in the 16 hp class. In addition three other records were to be broken in this class: the mile at 94.91 mph, the kilometre at 96.67 mph, and finally ten laps from a standing start were covered at 91.46 mph. In an attempt to reach 100 mph over the flying mile a big end broke, and as a result a piston came through the sump.

A month before the successful record-breaking attempt with the 16 hp car a very important event took place at the October Motor Show in London. This was the introduction of the C type, which quickly became known as the Prince Henry and eventually developed into the famous 30/98, possibly Britain's finest sporting car during the first quarter of the twentieth century. Production of the new model started in the following year. Initially around forty-five cars were produced, with the 3-litre 80 x 120 mm engine installed in the 9 ft 6 in chassis, which had a track of 4 ft 6 in. Later in the same year a 3½-litre engine replaced the earlier unit in a further batch of thirteen examples. The respected motoring journalist Laurence E. Pomeroy, son of the famous Vauxhall designer, later recalled: 'Unfortunately the 3 litre radiator had insufficient cooling area and this model was notorious for boiling if driven fast upon a summer's day. Nevertheless, this small, light car was tremendous fun to drive, and I remember as a boy many long journeys sitting in the dickey-seat of my father's two-seater.'

1912 saw Pomeroy elevated from Works Manager to the position of Chief Engineer, a long overdue appointment. On the competition front the company gained further laurels. In the Swedish trials of February 1912 Kidner drove the company's entry, the C-type Prince Henry. He was later described by Maurice Platt, Chief Engineer from 1953 to 1963, as being opinionated, inflexible, robustly extrovert, not particularly intelligent but a motor car enthusiast! Something of his character came through in this most gruelling event. The weather was excruciatingly cold with temperatures as low as -8°F but Kidner wore an ordinary motoring coat. In order to overcome the climatic difficulties he had installed a canvas hood which was raised from the dashboard to eye level so that the slipstream caused the snow to pass above his head. By drilling the floorboards, a certain amount of heat was allowed to rise, saving the Vauxhall's reckless driver from frostbite, a condition which affected many competitors in these very low temperatures. Percy Kidner arrived at the finish at Stockholm 1½ hours ahead of the nearest competitor. Unfortunately under the event's peculiar regulations he was deemed to be too far ahead to receive the award. However, he was given a victor's reception by the crowd in appreciation of his epic run, which was somewhat akin to an exploit in a *Boys' Own* magazine.

In June 1912 Vauxhall Motors took three 3-litre cars to Dieppe which they entered in the Coupe de l'Auto Voiturette. On this occasion success eluded the Luton team, with none of the cars finishing the race.

The price of an ex-works 3-litre Prince Henry chassis was £485 on its introduction. In both the First and Second World Wars the performance of the Luton-built product enhanced its reputation in the post-war years. 1912 saw the introduction of the 25 hp D type, which would remain in production until 1921 and is probably best known for its role as the army staff car of the First World War. Initially the D type was designed to take the heavy coachwork of the period. Power was provided by a 4-litre side valve engine (95 x 140 mm). The design of the engine was similar in many respects to the A type; however, the camshaft was driven by an internally toothed chain. The engine produced 50 bhp at 2000 rpm. The chassis had a wheelbase of 10 ft 10 in and although remembered as a tourer, many other types of body were fitted. Most examples were originally fitted from the factory with wire wheels although a few examples were supplied with discs. The new model was exactly what the company needed. By the end of 1912 production for the year had reached 300 cars. The B type was now rated at 35 hp. The chassis was popular, not only with the Romanoffs, but also with wealthier customers in the British Isles. Production of the B type was phased out in 1914 with the start of the First World War. Many of the bodies fitted to this chassis represented the finest of British coachwork at the time, although it is said that the six-cylinder B type was not one of Vauxhall's better designs.

In December 1913 production started of the 4-litre version of the 'Prince Henry'. In all, a total of 130 examples were produced over the coming months. The engine was a tuned version of the unit used in the D type. At this time the directors of Vauxhall were well aware of the increasing competition from such rivals as Sunbeam and Talbot.

Around this time, towards the end of 1912 and the beginning of 1913, Mr Joseph Higginson, perhaps best remembered as the inventor of the Autovac, contacted Vauxhall's directors as he was anxious to acquire a high performance car capable of outdistancing the competition at hill-climb events. Higginson was a leading amateur competitor at such events and had regularly driven a 13.6-litre La Buire 80 over the previous three years. He was also director of the Hollingdrake Motor Company of Stockport, Lancashire, who were the importers of the La Buire. By 1913 the La Buire 80 with its vast four-cylinder 80 bhp engine was fast becoming a dinosaur from another age. The result of Higginson's discussion with the directors was the 30/98 with a light body powered by the 4.5-litre engine (98 x 150 mm). The new car would go on to make 1913 the most successful year for Vauxhall Motors in terms of competition successes. On 13 May the new car appeared for the first time, when Higginson recorded the fastest time at the Lancashire Automobile Club's hill climb at Waddington Fell. At the Whitsun Brooklands meeting on 12 May the company entered a 1912 single-seater, which had originally been fitted with the 3-litre engine and had won the O'Gorman trophy again for the company in that year. Driven by A.J. Hancock, the car was not fitted with the 4.5-litre 30/98 engine. The car performed magnificently and only failed to win the Short Handicap by half a length. Unfortunately, shortly after this success, the meeting was abandoned because of rain.

On 24 May, at Aston Clinton in Buckinghamshire, the hill record was broken by A.J. Hancock driving one of the 1912 Coupe de l'Auto two-seater racing cars, in which the original 3-litre engine had been replaced by a 98 × 150 engine. The car was fitted with mudguards, running boards and headlights and still only tipped the scales at 17 cwt. Higginson's reward for changing to the new Vauxhall came on 8 June at Shelsby Walsh, when on his last run he climbed the hill in 55.2 seconds, a record which was not broken for eight years. The Coupe de l'Auto car, driven by A.J. Hancock, reinforced Vauxhall's reputation by putting in the quickest time at the Caerphilly hill climb on 19 June. A two-seater 3-litre was entered in that year's Coupe de l'Auto, which as in previous years was held in Boulogne in September. With A.J. Hancock driving, the car finished fourth behind two twin cam 16 valve Peugeots and a four-cylinder side-valve Sunbeam.

Production of the 30/98 slowly got under way and the first few cars were delivered in July 1913. The model's capabilities were underlined in the autumn of that year when an example put in a lap of 99.6 mph at Brooklands, where earlier Hancock, driving KN2, powered by the 4-litre engine, had broken six world records and two class records; after nine and a half hours driving a front spring shackle broke, robbing him of the twelve hour attempt.

1914 saw the company enter both the French Grand Prix held at Lyons and the Isle of Man TT. The cars were fitted with four-cylinder twin cam sixteen valve engines. The Grand Prix cars used a 4½-litre engine and the TT cars a 3-litre engine. Both events were a disaster for the company. The Grand Prix cars were driven by Hancock, Willie Watson, who was the company's agent for Liverpool, and American Ralph de Palma. None of the Vauxhall team got beyond the seventh lap because of fuel starvation, as a result of the air pressure in the fuel tanks being reduced. In the Isle of Man again three cars were entered. In this case they were driven by Hancock, Higginson and Watson. Both Watson's and Higginson's cars retired on the first lap with engine problems, while Hancock's car crashed on the second day, putting it out of the race.

With the advent of the First World War, foreigners living in France had to leave or face internment. With this in mind a young man, Clarence E. King, who had been living in France endeavouring to earn a living as a painter, wrote to Vauxhall Motors seeking employment. Born in Highbury Hill, North London, in 1888, he was educated at the local elementary school in Clapham Road. In the early 1900s his father, who was a pioneer Socialist and an upholsterer, had moved to the Anglers' Rest public house on the outskirts of Bedford. CEK, as he was always known, joined the Adams Manufacturing Company Limited in Bedford. Adams manufactured a range of motor cars from 1905 to 1914. Starting as a mechanic, King studied at night school like Pomeroy and was put in charge of the drawing office in December 1911. On 26 May 1912 he left Adams' Cars and moved to Paris, living in a garret on the Rue Campagne Premier. Obviously finding life very hard as a painter, he joined the Société Lorraine. Just before taking up regular employment again he married Kathleen Colls at the British Consulate in Paris. His late son Geoffrey always said he took the job with Société Lorraine because 'Mother liked to eat regularly'.

On returning to England with his new wife, King was given a job in the drawing office of Vauxhall Motors as Pomeroy's assistant. He remained with Vauxhall Motors until he retired from the Board in 1954 and was responsible for many successful designs.

Vauxhall's sporting activities continued throughout the spring and summer of 1914 until the beginning of the war with Germany on 4 August. As mentioned earlier, the D type proved the ideal army staff car during the conflict. In all, almost two thousand were manufactured. The Services used a number of makes, Rolls-Royce being favoured as the basis of armoured cars. The Royal Flying Corps used the 25 hp Crossley, while the Royal Naval Air Service favoured Clement-Talbots and the Sizaire-Berwicks. The Army also used the robust Ford Model T, the excellent Sunbeam 12/16, the 20 hp Daimler (which did not stand up well under the arduous conditions in which it had to operate), in addition to models from Napier, Siddeley-Deasy and Wolseley. The 25 hp Vauxhall D type was supplied in open tourer form and as an enclosed limousine. It has been said that the Vauxhall limousine was used by senior officers who could not get a Rolls-Royce, as the majority were bodied as armoured cars. In addition to the D type, Vauxhall Motors produced detonator caps for shells and a Pomeroy-designed V12 aircraft engine.

Throughout the war, Pomeroy kept experimenting with various ideas. These included experiments with camshaft design. At the end of the war in 1918 Pomeroy designed and built a low compression 3½-litre V12 engine. Owing to its very low compression ratio, the unit produced only 50 bhp. It is said that the engine ran with the smoothness of a turbine, but it never saw production. In the same year Pomeroy designed his replacement for the 30/98, the H type. The power unit featured an overhead camshaft with extensive use of aluminium. The single overhead camshaft was driven by three-throw eccentrics and operating two valves per cylinder. An aluminium block was used with wet liners, and the bore and stroke was 100 x 140 mm. It has been claimed that the engine would run up to possibly 3,500 rpm and produced around 120 bhp. The chassis of the H type had a longer wheelbase than the 30/98. Two H types were built in the spring of 1920. The first example competed in a number of sporting events, showing that the design had considerable promise. Both cars were later sold to members of the public.

Production of civilian models started again in 1919. At the beginning of the same year Laurence Pomeroy left for America as a result of family problems. He was accompanied by a woman friend, leaving behind his wife who suffered from alcoholism. Pomeroy's departure was without doubt a considerable blow. He had plans to produce the 30/98 in America but nothing came of these.

In November 1926 Laurence Pomeroy returned to England, joining the Daimler Company as Chief Engineer and acting as a consultant to the London General Omnibus Company. He brought with him to Daimler E.W. Hancock from Vauxhall (brother to A.J. Hancock). Pomeroy was responsible for a number of Daimler designs, culminating in the Straight Eight of May 1934. However, his greatest achievements while at Daimler were the introduction and popularization of the fluid flywheel and the introduction of the poppet valve Daimler engine.

In 1936 Pomeroy left Daimler, where he had been Managing Director since August 1929, and joined de Havilland Aircraft as General Manager of the engine division. In November 1938 he set up as a patent consultant in London, later joining H&M Hobson Aircraft and Motor Components Ltd, running their Midlands branch up to the time of his death on 27 May in 1941 at the age of fifty-seven, as the result of sudden and unexpected heart failure. Pomeroy is now best remembered for his brilliant designs at Vauxhall, his sharp wit and quick mind. (Referring to Rolls-Royce he had said that the Silver Ghost was a triumph of workmanship over design.)

When Laurence Pomeroy departed from Vauxhall in early 1919 production of the existing models, the D type and the 30/98, was slowly increasing as the factory geared up for production again. The D type sold nearly 600 examples in 1919, no doubt partly as a result of the excellent reputation the model had acquired in the conflict.

For the first time in over five years, a visit by the press was organized for 17 June. The party consisted of the major part of the motoring press and a considerable number of other press men. The press representatives met at St Pancras station in London, joining the 9.40 train to Luton. On arrival, the party was met by company representatives with new Vauxhall motor cars.

At the time of Pomeroy's departure, some in the motor industry thought that Vauxhall without Pomeroy would soon lose its pre-eminence in the field. While it was true that Pomeroy was Vauxhall, and vice versa, these prophets of doom considerably underrated the talents of Clarence Evelyn King.

The 100 M.P.H. CAR

A.J. Hancock at the wheel of the first 20 hp car to exceed 100 mph.

A late six-cylinder B type of 1914. Vintage points of interest are the low radiator, early electric lights and a more streamlined scuttle. This car was ordered by the House of Romanoff for use in St Petersburg.

Charles Frederick Sanderson behind the wheel of his Prince Henry, outside his home at Westcliff-on-Sea. The car is of about 1914 vintage. The registration number is JN4341.

Vauxhall's entry for the Coupe de l'Auto Voiturette held at Dieppe in June 1912. Both rear springs were shackled at either end, the axle being located by radius rods. The event was held over two days. Vauxhall entered three cars, driven by W. Watson (seen here in car no. 14), J. Lambert and A.J. Hancock. The Vauxhalls were the fastest car in their class. Hancock held the lead after five laps (about 240 miles). However, all Vauxhalls retired before the end of the race: Watson with a broken big end bolt, Lambert with big end trouble and Hancock with a broken piston.

One of the Vauxhall cars for the French Grand Prix of 1914. For the first time in the event's history there was a limit to engine size – 4½ litres. Unfortunately the cars suffered from the same problems as in the Tourist Trophy, and started in the Grand Prix in a far from finished condition. Hancock retired on the first lap with a broken piston, Watson had carburettor troubles and Ralph de Palma did better but was unable to finish the race.

The Pomeroy-designed 16 valve twin ohc, four-cylinder, 4½-litre engine, as used in the 1914 French Grand Prix car.

One of the IOM TT cars of 1914, which used a 3-litre version of the twin-cam engine. A.J. Hancock is seen behind the wheel with his mechanic Gibbs.

Higginson's machine for the 1914 TT race. The 1914 TT was a bad race for Vauxhall; Watson and Higginson retired with engine problems in the first lap. On the second day Hancock and Gibbs met disaster when their car turned over on the mountain.

Watson and his mechanic pose for the camera.

A Vauxhall D-type staff car of the First World War.

The D type was often fitted with a limousine body, as seen here. Note the types of tread pattern on the front tyres. As in the Second World War the Luton product was a favourite of all ranks.

THE OFFICIAL ORGAN OF THE MOTOR TRADE ASSOCIATION AND THE AGENTS SECTION LTD.

# MOTOR COMMERCE

VOL. I. NO. 1.       MAY 17, 1919.       ONE SHILLING.

## ONE MAKE WAS SUPEREXCELLENT IN WAR

IN a long article that appeared on April 5th, *The Times* described the 25-h.p. Vauxhall as "the most successful of staff vehicles . . . with the seal of official success set on it." Mr. H. Massac Buist pointed out in the *Morning Post*, dated February 15th, that "throughout the war the four-cylinder Vauxhall cars have proved the most generally satisfactory of any British make for staff service."

IT is, in fact, everywhere known (although one cannot expect it to be everywhere admitted) that the 25-h.p. Vauxhall did better at the front than any other car, and was actually "the finest car on active service." This strong argument of war superiority will repay continual and energetic employment by Vauxhall agents, for it is an epitome of well-nigh all that can be said about automobile excellence.

**VAUXHALL MOTORS LIMITED, LUTON, BEDFORDSHIRE**
Telephone : LUTON 466-7-8-9.       Telegrams : CARVAUX LUTON

This advertisement from *Motor Commerce*, 17 May 1919, is self-explanatory.

The D-type engine from the exhaust side. The unit proved very reliable in service and was later developed in the OD unit by C.E. King.

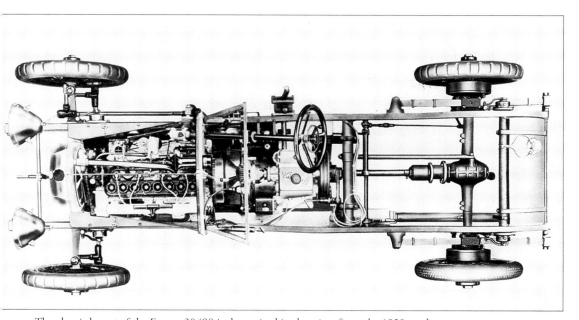

The chassis layout of the E-type 30/98 is shown in this plan view from the 1920 catalogue.

A view of the H-type engine, Pomeroy's final design for Vauxhall Motors. The design dated from 1918. The engine's dimensions of 100 mm x 150 mm were identical to the 1914 Grand Prix engine. There were two valves per cylinder and a single overhead camshaft. Two cars were built in 1920, both being eventually sold to members of the public. It is said that Pomeroy's swansong had a performance which was superior to either the E or OE 30/98.

Jack Payne was foreman of the running shop. He is seen here behind the wheel of one of the two prototype H types. He carried out the testing of Vauxhall's first four-wheel braking system on the H type. He was an excellent driver, putting up a good performance in the H type at Aston Hill on 16 July 1921, and in the following year, when he drove one of the Vauxhall TT cars to third place on the Isle of Man.

# 1920–1929: ENTER
# GENERAL MOTORS

June 1922 was a particularly busy month for Vauxhall Motors. During the first week of May the Vauxhall Tourist Trophy car was shown for the first time at Brooklands. The design featured a 3-litre twin-cam sixteen valve engine designed by H.R. Ricardo, with the chassis and brakes by C.E. King. The engine had a bore and stroke of 85 × 132 mm. A glowing report appeared in *The Autocar* of 13 May. It was noted in practice that, despite the fact that the car was being run in, lap speeds were nevertheless quite good, with speeds from 88 to just over 90 mph. For this first outing the car was painted a very light green, although by the date of the race all three Vauxhall cars had been painted red. For the race they were numbered 2, 5 and 8. No. 2 was driven by Matthew Park, who was foreman in the repair shop. His riding mechanic was E.W. Pugh. Car no. 5 was driven by 'Jock' Payne accompanied by A.G. Blackborough, and in car no. 8 was Ernest Swain, who was the road test department foreman, accompanied by his mechanic O.G. Walker.

Although the Vauxhall entries driven by Park and Swain retired during the race, 'Jock' Payne driving car no. 5 finished third behind the Bentley of F.C. Clement. Commenting in *The Autocar* on 7 July, B.H. Davies wrote: 'I am not sure that one of the Vauxhalls may not have been absolutely the fastest car in the Tourist Trophy. But it would have been a miracle if a car newly designed, recently completed, and hardly tested had won . . . I do not think there are many cars of this size which could keep them in sight when every detail is right.' History would prove Mr Davies correct in his assumption, as one of the cars was timed at Brooklands in 1926 reaching 112.42 mph. A further example became the Vauxhall Villier's Special. Driven by Raymond Mays (later of BRM fame) this much modified car became very successful in sprints and hill climbs. The three TT cars were the last racing cars produced by Vauxhall.

At the beginning of June the OD type went into production. This was King's updated version of the D type, sometimes referred to as the 23/60. The 3969 cc engine acquired overhead valves and a detachable cylinder head. In addition the engine was fitted with a Lanchester crankshaft damper. The brakes continued to be fitted to rear wheels only apart from a transmission brake. Like all Vauxhalls prior to the R-type 20/60, braking was not a strong point.

After the First World War there was an economic slump which caused the demise of many motor vehicle manufacturers. Very simply, there were too few buyers for the numerous makes and models on offer. With this in mind the company introduced the 2297 cc four-cylinder M type. The side valve engine featured a detachable alloy head and produced 43 bhp, giving the new car a top speed of around 55–57 mph depending on the type of bodywork fitted. Prices started at £650.

In December 1922 the first OE 30/98 was delivered to its new owner. The OE was King's modernized version of Pomeroy's design. The new car had a 4 in longer wheelbase and the chassis was of heavier gauge steel. The slightly wider body incorporated a number of genuine improvements with regard to fixtures and fittings. The main difference, compared with its predecessor, was its overhead valve engine, which produced around 112 bhp. Probably the most radical piece of design was the duralumin connecting rods. This material had been used for airframe construction during the war, and the patent was held by Vickers. The OE engine proved to be durable and generally trouble free. As with the OD engine the new unit had a very handsome appearance. With his new overhead valve engines King started a tradition: all future Vauxhall engines, with the exception of Alex Taub's side valve flat twelve engine for the Churchill tank, were ohv designs, and apart from the company's single overhead cam units designed by John Alden and introduced in 1967, they used push rods. It is also a fact that, over the years, the push rod Vauxhall engine, with a few exceptions, was the most durable in its field.

Production of the new OE 30/98 gradually got under way during the first seven months of 1923. The cars were capable of on one hand performing the duties of a fast touring car and on the other proving to be competitive in sporting events. The OE was still fitted with two-wheel brakes. Although this might seem incredible today, one has to remember that at this time traffic generally was very light.

In 1922 the only Vauxhall motor-cycle was designed by Major Halford, who later designed the Napier Sabre engine which powered the Hawker Tempest fighter aircraft. By 1923 two machines had been built. However, production difficulties are blamed for the design never getting into production. A further six frames and twelve engines were constructed before the project came to a halt. Had the design gone into production it would have been one of the most advanced of its period and probably one of the most expensive! When the company decided not to proceed employees were invited to submit bids for the completed machines or for spare parts. One bike was purchased for £45 by a company draughtsman and another by a Vauxhall apprentice. Only one machine survives today.

By the 1920s Clarence Evelyn King's position in life had changed considerably. The once impoverished engineer/artist, who in 1911 had been a member of the Independent Labour Party, was now living at Tower House, Kingston, Hertfordshire, set in 16 acres of land. At the time of the introduction of the OE 30/98 in 1923 his salary was £1,200 a year, rising to £1,500 in the following year.

In America General Motors was, and is still today, the largest corporation involved in motor vehicle production. For many years Ford dominated the low-price field with their Model T. General Motors had been formed in 1908 by W.C. Durant. As the name implies, his idea was to collect together a number of companies, each with a limited degree of independence. By 1918 the group had the market fairly well covered on the motor car front. At the top end were the excellent products of Cadillac and Buick. At the other end was the cheap and cheerful Chevrolet 490, which had been designed to compete with Henry Ford's Model T. The Chevrolet failed to match the Ford in either quality or price.

On 19 June 1911 General Motors organized the General Motors Export Company to sell their products in foreign markets. The Buick car had been sold in Britain since 1909, and from 1910 for a number of years the Buick chassis was available with English coachwork. Between 1910 and 1914 these English-bodied Buicks were sold as Bedford-Buicks. General Motors had premises at Hendon in North London, which from 1923 were used for the assembly of Chevrolet trucks; for many years they were also used for assembling the trim on General Motors cars of North American origin for the British market. From the 1920s up to the outbreak of the Second World War in 1939 the Buick in particular was popular with the more affluent motorists. The majority of these cars were imported from Canada, which as part of the British Empire enjoyed what was known at the time as Imperial Preference. This meant that heavy import duties, which were applied to all vehicles imported from foreign countries throughout most of this period, were avoided.

General Motors was considering expansion into Europe at the end of the First World War. In 1919 a bid was made for Citroën. However, the French government of the day was very reluctant to allow a major French manufacturer to be taken over by a foreign rival, and partly as a result of this attitude General Motors withdrew from the negotiations. During 1924–25 discussions took place with the Austin Motor Company of Longbridge, Birmingham. In the spring of 1925 the factory was inspected. In the following July, after a further visit, a committee of senior General Motors staff recommended a take-over of Austin. On 11 September, however, the offer was withdrawn as agreement could not be reached on Austin's estimated value of its assets. It was felt that the plant was in poor condition and its management weak. Immediately afterwards negotiations took place to purchase Vauxhall Motors. The deal was made public in November, General Motors paying $2,575,291 (approximately £650,000 at the then current exchange rate). Many people were not pleased with the take-over of one of Britain's most respected motor manufacturers by a giant American company. This was reflected in the fact that the words General Motors were not used in the advertising and publicity of Vauxhall's products until comparatively recently.

As far as the general public was concerned, Vauxhall continued very much as before. Some of the old guard left, but C.E. King stayed on (as Chief Engineer), as did many of the employees. The author's late friend Geoffrey King, who was the son of CEK, said that his father invited fellow engineers who were already with the company in 1925 to 'join in tackling the problems that lay ahead'.

The output of motor cars from Luton in 1925 was 1,400 vehicles. By this time some 1,800 staff were employed.

Shortly before the takeover by General Motors, the company announced the new S type, also known as the 25/70. This was the company's only sleeve valve design. The 3.8-litre engine was said at the time to be exceptionally smooth running. Although beautifully made, the S type was expensive, a limousine costing in the region of £1,700. The chassis alone weighed 1 ton 11½ cwt. In addition to a limousine body tourers and saloons were also available: effectively the wrong car at the wrong time. Production ceased in 1928, by which time fifty had been sold.

The production of the other pre-General Motors Vauxhalls ceased in 1926 and 1927. The OD 23/60 finished in 1926, followed by the OE 30/98 and the LM 14/40 in 1927. During these final years of pre-GM Vauxhall production, success and headline-making continued, a typical example being at the 1926 Easter Brooklands Meeting, when Jack Barclay, later better known for his Rolls-Royce/Bentley showrooms in Berkeley Square, driving a TT Vauxhall racing car, was forced up the Byfleets banking and went into a high speed skid, eventually coming down, turning around and travelling backwards at some 80 mph. Barclay kept the engine running and continued the race. Later he brought the car out again and won, lapping at nearly 112 mph.

In 1927 the last 30/98s were constructed. For the last two years of production a higher radiator line was used, in keeping with the fashion of the time. Larger brake drums on the front axle were a result of the Vauxhall hydraulic braking system which had originally been introduced on the sleeve valve 25/70. When new the system could give impressive results on both models, but in service the system was less satisfactory: leaks could develop because of the use of leather seals. However, these final models were the first Vauxhalls to have brakes that, when working properly, were up to the vehicles' performance; it would be another ten years before Vauxhall fitted a modern reliable hydraulic braking system. In the case of the dual system fitted to G models of 1937, they were at least thirty years ahead of most other manufacturers' designs.

As a result of increasing competition the final 30/98s proved difficult to sell. As a result Jack Barclay bought the remaining nine cars, which he sold at reduced prices throughout the spring and summer of 1928. The final car was offered for sale in the autumn of that year at £875. What a bargain!

The company's new 23/60 was the combined effort of C.E. King and General Motors. The new design was exactly the kind of robust motor car that was popular in parts of the British Empire. If the R type had a problem in its home country, it was its low price and American appearance. When introduced at Olympia in the autumn of 1927 at £495, the R type represented a genuine quality car at a very fair price; a far more practical proposition than the sleeve valve S type at £1,625. Ventures such as the S type would have finished Vauxhall in the early years of the new decade, as Argyll had found out and Arrol-Johnston was about to. With the arrival of General Motors new machinery was installed and, over a period of years, the works were enlarged and extra staff were employed.

For the British motorist who still wanted a coach-built body on his new R type, Vauxhall's traditional coach-builders, Grosvenor, were happy to oblige. Some of the designs were particularly elegant. Depending on the weight of the car and the body chosen, the R type had a top speed approaching 70 mph and would cruise happily in the mid-50s.

Sales were up from 1,388 in 1925 to 1,645 in 1927. The year 1929 saw further improvements to the design. The engine capacity was enlarged to 2.9 litres by increasing the bore size from 73 to 75 mm. The cast-iron pistons were replaced by aluminium pistons and the ride was improved with the fitting of the latest type Hertford dampers. Following the styling trends of the time, the front wings were changed to give a more domed appearance and again the height of the bonnet line was increased. Completing the changes were larger headlights. The most handsome design of the revised range was the Velox fabric saloon by Grosvenor. Wire wheels reappeared on some models. Vauxhall was still far from being a mass producer in the accepted sense of the word: even by 1930 the annual production was only 1,277 cars, just 1 per cent of the market.

1929 also saw the introduction of a new limousine, the Westminster, which sold for £705 and offered good performance for the period as it was fitted with a 5.1:1 rear axle ratio. Throughout the coming decade the company offered an inexpensive limousine much in the same way as Austin did from the late 1940s through to the '60s. By this time Leslie Walton was the company's chairman. His colleague, Percy Kidner, had left, taking with him A.J. Hancock and Frank Beecher. Hancock had been works manager and for many years Frank Beecher was the sales manager under the old company. With the help of Hancock and Beecher, Kidner launched a successful car sales and service organization in Oxford. In later years the late Geoffrey King was told by Maurice Platt how Walton lost several close friends because of his decision to stay on at Luton. Some of this anti-American feeling had been whipped up by the proprietor of *Motor* magazine, Edmund Dangerfield. As a result of the strong criticism which had been published in this magazine, all advertising ceased for a number of years.

By the late '20s Vauxhall Motors was being run on a day-to-day basis by an American, Bob Evans. Evans was responsible, among other things, for building and equipping a new die-and-press shop. He was also an expert in the art of shaping steel and would personally demonstrate the use of machinery and the skills required to obtain the perfect draw with pressings. September 1929 saw the arrival of Charles John Bartlett who came from GM's Hendon depot on the recommendation of James Mooney, the chairman of GM's overseas committee. Bartlett replaced Bob Evans and over the coming years would prove himself to be one of the most far-sighted managing directors in the British motor industry. Under Bartlett's leadership Vauxhall's market share rapidly increased, and by 1938 the company had 11 per cent of the British market, having produced 60,111 cars.

Bartlett was born at Bibury, Gloucestershire, in 1889. The Bartletts were a modest west country family. After leaving the local school he attended Bath Technical College, where he received training in business methods, specializing in accountancy. In 1914 Bartlett enlisted in the Devonshire Regiment, but was wounded at the battle of Loos in the early part of the First World War; he later served in the Middle East. At the time of his demobilization he had reached the rank of sergeant. On leaving the army he joined General Motors Limited at Hendon, where he was an account clerk. Because of his flair for administration and financial matters he was appointed Managing Director in 1926 – remarkable progress in only eight years.

Maurice Platt said of CJB (as Bartlett was generally referred to) that despite his promotions he never lost his simple and sturdy democratic approach to industrial management. He had a sense of humour and a strong will and did a great deal to break down the barriers between management and the shop floor. His greatest contribution to industrial relations was his Management Advisory Committee which was set up in 1941. Under the scheme the factory was split into twenty areas; each area had a representative elected by secret ballot. Every four weeks these representatives, who were a majority on the Management Advisory Committee, met with Bartlett to discuss outstanding problems. The representatives automatically retired after three years but were eligible for re-election. In addition to shop floor representation on the committee, there were also six representatives from the company's management. The result of Bartlett's enlightened ideas was that Vauxhall Motors had the most strike-free factory in the British motor industry for many years.

From 1925 to 1940 the company acquired the services of a number of talented individuals, of whom perhaps the most important was Arthur Francis Palmer Phillips, joining Charles Bartlett from Hendon. For twenty-four years, University-educated Palmer Phillips held the post of Sales Director. His shrewd marketing was a major part of the phenomenal growth of the company during the 1930s. Palmer Phillips was in his element when hitting back at critics of the company's products, especially if they had made the great mistake of referring to them as 'Yankee rubbish'. He would simply point out the facts and demolish their case. Even today the British car enthusiast tends to overlook the older Vauxhall in favour of many rival products whose engineering quality was very often decidedly inferior. Conversely the Bedford truck and bus remain extremely popular with restorers of historic commercial vehicles, possibly a matter of past direct personal involvement in the haulage or bus industries rather than being just an enthusiast – as is often the case with the classic car owner.

A stylish six-light saloon body, a stiffer chassis, hydraulic shock absorbers and a mechanical fuel pump were some of the main improvements made to the T type of 1930. In addition chromium plating was now standard although wire wheels remained an optional extra. The number of models offered on the T type was reduced from eleven to six, in addition to the availability of a chassis for open bodies and a chassis for closed bodies for the motorist who wished to have a chassis bodied by a coach builder of his choice. The new ex-works bodies for 1930 were the handsome Kingston coupé, the Hurlingham two-seater sports and the Richmond saloon.

The 1930 cars were praised for their refinement and quality of finish, excellent brakes and useful gear ratios. Some road testers thought the steering was slightly low geared; one well-known authority on Vauxhalls of this period commented to the author that a well-restored Hurlingham was more fun to drive in modern conditions that an OE 30/98 because of, in particular, the vastly superior brakes and general ease of control.

The year 1931 was a momentous one for the company. The first true General Motors-inspired car, the Cadet, was in production and the company's new commercial vehicle, the Bedford, appeared. Both events would totally transform Vauxhall Motors from a low-volume manufacturer to a mass producer of value-for-money cars and commercial vehicles. Although the prices of the new ranges were extremely competitive, the quality of construction and engineering remained among the best in the industry. The reasons for this were two-fold. The chief engineer, C.E. King, was without doubt a very talented man and since 1925 had built up one of the best design teams in Britain. Secondly, the company had access to General Motors' considerable expertise regarding the manufacture and marketing of motor cars.

The reason for General Motors wishing to expand overseas was a direct result of the problems of selling American vehicles abroad. Many dollar-poor nations imposed high tariffs and severe quotas on imported American vehicles. This was particularly true of Western Europe. Countries such as Great Britain, France, Germany and Italy produced about three-quarters of the vehicles they required. Vauxhall lost money in the first few years after General Motors' take-over, and it became clear to senior management that the corporation would have to develop a smaller car if they were to capture a greater percentage of the British market. James Mooney was Vice-President in charge of General Motors Export Companies at this time and he was keen to press ahead as rapidly as possible, regarding Vauxhall as a bridgehead to overseas production. Alfred Sloan, however, who was GM President and Chief Executive Officer, took the view that a slow and cautious approach was preferable. On 26 January 1928 the executive committee of General Motors had debated the question of the desirability of manufacturing General Motors' vehicles abroad. The questions were: was it necessary to manufacture in Europe? should Vauxhall be expanded or written off as a bad investment? could a modified Chevrolet be exported from the USA to compete with European cars in their home territories? The final question the committee had to decide upon was what to do in Germany, where the corporation already had an assembly plant in Berlin. On the German question, Mooney was in favour of expanding the Berlin assembly, while Sloan preferred joining up with an existing German manufacturer. The committee met again on 29 March, with a further meeting on 12 April, when the question regarding the manufacture of a small car in England and Germany was discussed at length.

Many members of the committee were of the opinion that export organizations should not get involved in overseas manufacture and should limit activities to the export and selling of American products overseas. Alfred Sloan was interested in the idea that a modified small bore Chevrolet would avoid the taxation burden that was placed on large bore engines in Britain and Germany; he was of the opinion that if this course of action was taken it might not be necessary to develop a new small car at Vauxhall or start production in Germany, and in any event the corporation would have a design available should it be decided that overseas production was still viable.

Discussions continued throughout the rest of 1928. In these discussions James Mooney pushed for the expansion of Vauxhall Motors. He pointed out that the Chevrolet cost 75 per cent more in world markets than it did in the United States and that the purchaser in world markets had approximately only 60 per cent of the money of a US buyer to pay for it. Thus the car would end up in a relatively high price bracket. His argument centred around the fact that the British Empire covered 38 per cent of the world markets outside the United States and Canada and therefore there was great export potential. General Motors had already started a manufacturing programme which they proposed to expand by adding another model: this was the King-designed R type, a 'middle-market' car as opposed to Vauxhall's previous models, which were designed to compete against the more expensive cars of their day. The new model he was referring to was the Cadet, which was introduced in October 1930. Mooney also pointed out, in his case for the expansion of Vauxhall, that they had a large and growing distribution system in Britain and an investment in the Vauxhall plant that had to be safeguarded. Mooney was successful in advocating a smaller, lower-priced model, designed by Vauxhall.

On the question of continental production, Sloan's idea won the day. On 18 January 1929 the group purchased a majority shareholding in Opel. At that time Opel was the largest German manufacturer of motor vehicles: in 1928 their total output was 43,000 vehicles. In October 1931 General Motors purchased the remaining 20 per cent of shares from the Opel company.

In 1930 the production of Chevrolet trucks and cars was moved from Hendon to Luton. With the introduction of the Bedford range in May 1931 General Motors' fortunes improved very rapidly in Britain. However, the sales of the new Cadet were disappointing, as were the sales of the existing T range. As a result, Alfred Sloan appointed a committee in the early part of 1932, instructing them to visit Britain and report and submit recommendations on Vauxhall's programme of models. The committee was led by Albert Bradley, who was vice-president of finance. The committee reported back to Sloan, recommending that the current range of Vauxhall cars be discontinued, to be followed by a smaller, lighter six-cylinder car and later a small lower horse-power four-cylinder car.

Bradley and his committee were correct in their diagnosis. The new models, the Light Six of 1933 and the Ten of 1938, were not only the best in their class in terms of design and refinement, they were also highly successful in terms of sales. In 1933 Vauxhall produced 9,949 cars; the following year this increased to 20,227. By 1936 Vauxhall recorded a profit for the year of £1.1 million. General Motors' long term investment at Luton was producing good results. These results were due to the long-term planning which was typical of GM. Unlike British firms, who very often went for short-term gains and pandered far too much to the shareholder, General Motors thought further ahead and consequently reaped the gains.

During the late '20s General Motors enlarged the production facilities, installed new machinery and gradually increased the staff at Vauxhall Motors. Not only was there an increase in shop floor workers but also a new team of engineers had joined the company. In 1929 the position of assistant chief engineer was taken by Harold Drew, who had joined General Motors from Sunbeam in 1925. Drew had worked in the Sunbeam drawing office under the gifted Louis Coatalen. He was responsible for developing the original range of Vauxhall/Bedford engines which were introduced with the Vauxhall Cadet and the Bedford truck range. Harold Drew remained Clarence E. King's assistant until 1953, and their partnership proved to be extremely productive.

The date is 1920 or 1921. The rather vintage-looking body was known as Armidale – referring to the purchaser. The chassis is the reliable D type. Notice the lack of weather protection for the chauffeur and the blinds in the rear quarters. The body is by Grosvenor.

The following sequence of photographs shows the factory as it was in 1920: this is the finished stores. When the press visited the works in 1919 they were impressed with the general layout.

The laboratory was presided over by Mr J.B. Hoblyn FIC, ARCS. It is recorded that Mr Hoblyn mixed and dispensed the cocktails when the press visited the factory in 1919!

The sawmills.

The toolroom.

The old fitting shop.

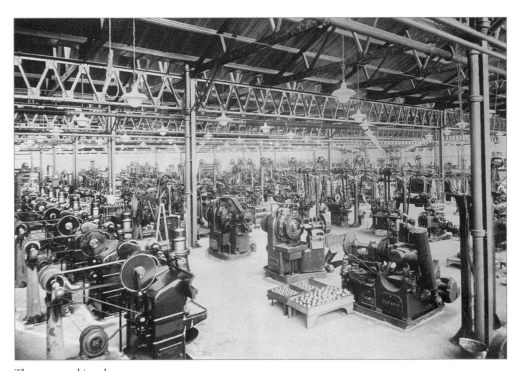

The new machine shop.

Mr Kidner's office.

Two views of one of the closed cars built on the E-type 30/98 chassis that Vauxhall Motors had on their stand at the 1920 Olympia Motor Show. Although Vauxhall catalogued Weymann-bodied saloons in 1927, the combination of a big four-cylinder engine and vintage coachwork was not a good idea. Very high noise levels were a problem. This example is certainly very handsome.

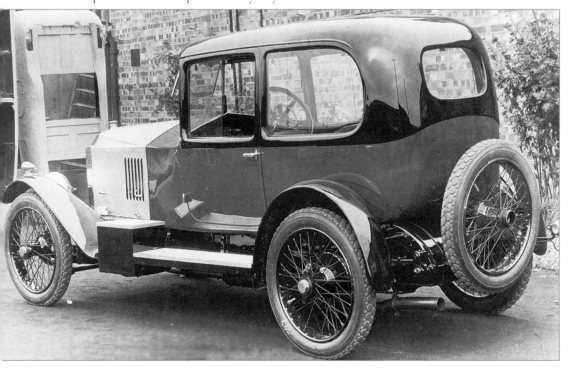

The Vauxhall motor-cycle was one of the most advanced designs of the early 1920s. Had it gone into production it would also have been one of the most expensive. This side view shows the engine and magneto. The design's four-cylinder engine had a bore and stroke of 67 mm; the output was around 30 bhp. The four cylinders were air-cooled, each cylinder being separate. The head was fixed and the two valves per cylinder were in a vertical position in the cylinder head. Wick lubrication was provided for the plain bearings that supported the rocker arms. The lightweight pistons and H-section connecting rods weighed 20.5 oz each. Three ball-bearings were used to support the two-piece crankshaft. Unlike the Vauxhall car of the period the engine used splash lubrication with connecting rod dippers in a wet sump. The drive to the rear wheel was via a 6 in multi-plate clutch made up of alternate steel and bronze plates. Motor car influence was shown in the use of a three-speed gearbox with shaft drive. The use of 7 in expanding brakes was another advanced idea in 1922. Six-volt coil ignition was used. A very robust duplex cradle frame helped to give the design excellent riding characteristics. The top speed was 82 mph and 70 mpg could be obtained when cruising at 50 mph.

Rear three-quarters view showing the shaft drive and construction of the rear hub.

Front three-quarters view showing the neat lines for the period and the layout of the front suspension.

A selection of photographs showing some of the styles of coachwork fitted to the D-type chassis in about 1921. This is an Arundel saloon with 'V' front. The body is by Grosvenor, and this type of coachwork was referred to as 'all-weather'.

Front three-quarters view of a Westminster saloon. The oval rear window was used on a number of Grosvenor designs of the period.

Offside three-quarters view of a Cavendish coupé – dickey up, October 1921. This is a Grosvenor-built three-quarter cabriolet. The hood folded down giving the owner the thrills of open-air motoring.

Windsor saloon with 'V' front. The more rounded look of this Grosvenor design gave the car a more modern appearance. Notice that there is only one door on the offside. This was quite a common practice among coachbuilders in the early 1920s.

Three-quarters front view of a Salisbury limousine. This is another Grosvenor design on nice vintage lines.

Three-quarters front view of Mr Gillett's saloon: the coachbuilder is unknown. Notice the single central door on this design.

Of all the amateur drivers who drove Vauxhall 30/98s in the early 1920s the most successful was Humphrey Cooke. His car was known as *Rouge et Noir*. The first of the two photographs shows the car in its original state, on 2 December 1921. The second photograph shows the car with its streamlined body, which was fitted in 1922. With its new body Cooke's success continued, although it is claimed that the car was not noticeably faster.

The bodywork on the E-type 30/98 ranged from the cut down example shown, obviously intended for competition work, to the rather ugly example below.

This rather bulbous body was fitted to the 1921 Olympia Show car. It featured a disappearing hood.

Two examples of two-seater bodies by Grosvenor on the E-type 30/98 chassis. The first photograph was taken on 6 July 1921. Both are nice examples of their type.

A wonderful line-up of D types and the new smaller M type identified by its disc wheels, possibly at Grosvenor's.

The M type was introduced at the 1921 Olympia Motor Show. The handsome little tourer shown here was displayed on the Vauxhall Motors stand. This photograph was taken on 2 November 1921.

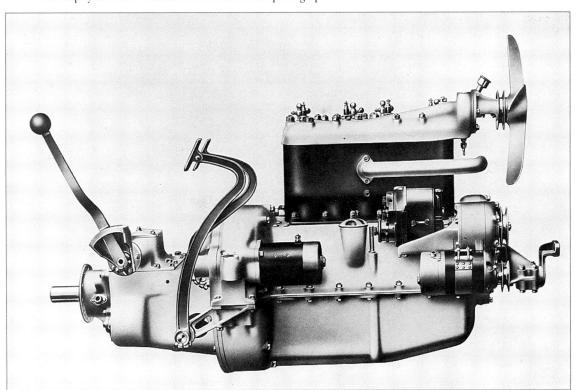

M-type engine, offside view; notice the extensive use of aluminium castings. The unit was the last Vauxhall car engine to use side valves.

*The 14-40 h.p. VAUXHALL-GRAFTON COUPE-CABRIOLET*
*(For description, see back)*

The 14/40 (M-type) Grafton coupé cabriolet, as illustrated in a Vauxhall catalogue of the period. The body is the work of Grosvenor, Vauxhall's house coachbuilder.

An OE 30/98 engine, photographed some years after it left the Luton works. SU carburettors have been fitted in place of the original up-draught Zenith and non-standard front brakes have also been fitted. The OE was introduced in 1923.

Also new in 1923 was the OD 23/60 which replaced the D type. Front brakes didn't arrive on the OD or OE types until 1925.

This is an S-type sports saloon with bodywork by Grosvenor. The wellbase wheels indicate 1927.

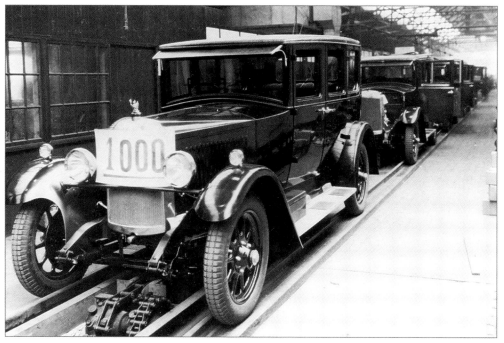

A selection of bodies were fitted to the R-type 20/60, which was in production from 1928 to 1930. The engine featured duralumin connecting rods, like all other C.E. King-designed engines of the 1920s. The brakes had 132 parts between the brake cable and shoes. They were very effective for their time and were the best brakes yet fitted to a Vauxhall. Although steps were taken to reduce costs where necessary, for example with steel pressings rather than alloy casting, the cars were very much a quality product. The front car here is the thousandth example to be produced.

When introduced, the 20/60 was only fitted with artillery wheels, which didn't help its appearance. This is the Princeton tourer.

The Melton two-seater with Rudge Whitworth wire wheels.

# 1930–1940: A Time for Expansion

By 1930 the production of Chevrolets had moved to Luton, and both the LQ truck range and the AC car chassis were in production. Sales of the Chevrolet car were very low as the engine was penalized by the British taxation system. Although the Bedford range, announced in April 1931, was launched at the height of the depression, success was immediate. The Bedford recipe for success, offering excellent value for money combined with quality engineering, was the formula also used for the new Vauxhall Cadet, introduced in the October of the previous year. The new model was part of General Motors' policy of moving Vauxhall into the volume market. Unlike its successor, the Light Six, the Cadet was of British appearance. At the time of its production, 1930–33, it was described as a car which sold at a low price with very full equipment and excellent coachwork. The standard model for the home market was powered by a six-cylinder ohv engine of 2048 cc, which was rated at 16.9 hp with a tax of £17. The unit was fitted with a four-bearing crankshaft, with ignition by coil and battery. Power output was 42 bhp at 3300 rpm.

The home market model was known as the VY. An export version, the VX, was fitted with the 3.2 litre 26.33 hp engine, which was also used in the company's new Bedford range. This unit was a close derivative of the original Cast Iron Wonder Chevrolet unit: although the bore and stroke was the same at 3$\frac{5}{16}$ x 3$\frac{3}{4}$, the 3180 cc engine had certain important improvements, notably a four-bearing crankshaft instead of Chevrolet's three-bearing design, and full pressure lubrication rather than Chevrolet's primitive splash lubrication. The larger engine developed 44 bhp at 2400 rpm. Both engines were of particularly neat appearance and even today look surprisingly modern. The use of all-leather trim for the car's interior showed that General Motors realized that the British motorist expected this feature in cars of this price class. American design was evident in the original 1931 models, which had 6 volt electrics and a three-speed gearbox; the Bendix-type brakes also showed American influence. The 17 hp saloon was initially priced at £280 and was capable of reaching 65 mph.

Throughout the '30s the company offered a wide range of coachbuilt designs from well-known coach builders of the day, such as Grosvenor, Salmons, Grose and Martin Walter. These designs were illustrated in the company's attractive catalogues of the period. For 1932 a number of improvements and changes were made to the Cadet. These included a change to 12 volt electrics, the replacement of the original Bishop cam-and-lever type steering by a Males-Weller cam-and-lever design. Another change was the use of larger hubs. However, the model's greatest claim to fame was the introduction of Britain's first Syncro-Mesh (original rendering) gearbox. The system was fitted to second and third gears. Syncromesh had been first introduced by GM's Cadillac division in 1929 on their model 341, and was the work of Earl A. Thompson, whose brother owned a Cadillac agency. Thompson took out a patent in 1922, and demonstrated his invention to Cadillac's Swedish-born chief engineer, Ernest Seaholm, who was suitably impressed. Unfortunately General Motors' New Devices Committee did not possess Seaholm's foresight on this occasion. When introduced by Cadillac in 1929, the syncromesh gearbox enabled many motorists to change gear cleanly for the first time. In the case of the Cadet the same was true. However, despite the Vauxhall company's excellent reputation for quality, sales were limited because of the British taxation system, which resulted in the Cadet owner having to pay £17 motor tax per year.

The 1933 models received chromium-plated flutes and a dull chromium-plated stoneguard, bringing the model in line with the new Light Six.

For 1931 the T-type had its engine enlarged to 3317 cc and was called the 'Silent 80'. In 1932 the flutes were chromium-plated and wire wheels were fitted as standard. The 80 never received a syncromesh gearbox. Although at the time eclipsed by the new Cadet, the 80 and its predecessors remain very underrated motor cars. At the Motor Show in Olympia in 1931, Grosvenor exhibited their very handsome Newmarket saloon. In many ways this represented the passing of another phase in the history of the Vauxhall motor car.

The R and T types had been advertised in Australia as 'a sincere attempt to meet Australia's needs'. Unfortunately they were simply too expensive, despite the use of locally built Holden bodies. The total production for the period 1927–31 was 721 units. Of these, 388 were tourers and 300 were saloons. It is also noticeable that production fell sharply after 1928. In New Zealand the price of an R-type saloon was £785, which was a lot of money in the late '20s.

During the first two years of Cadet production the numbers from Luton stayed below 4,000. By 1935, 26,240 Vauxhall cars were produced, out of a total production of 48,000 vehicles. The reason for this transformation was the new Light Six range, which provided the British motorist with a compact well-finished car which came in the 12 and 14 hp tax brackets, was economical to operate and very reasonably priced.

At the time of the introduction of the A-type Light Six in 1933, the horsepower tax was £1 per taxable unit. In 1935 this was reduced to 75p per taxable unit and finally in 1939 increased to £1.25, in today's money. Unfortunately, very little of this money was spent on British roads, much to the frustration of the British motorist. The result of this misguided tax system was the 'pint-sized' six of the early '30s. Many manufacturers added a couple of extra cylinders to their small four-cylinder engines in order to get over the problem of gear changing before the syncromesh gearbox and the pre-selector gear change became more common. Added to a poorly designed six-cylinder engine was very low gearing; this was a recipe for disaster, as many owners of Wolseleys, Triumphs, Austins, Crossleys, Morrises, Standards, Singers and Lanchesters discovered to their cost.

Prior to the launch of the Light Six in June 1933, the Luton works had been extensively modernized at a cost of £50,000. Two reports appeared in *The Motor* and *The Autocar* concerning the improvements and modernization that had taken place at Luton under General Motors. The first of these appeared in *The Motor* magazine in 1931. The article informed the reader that production was then 500 vehicles per week and that the new Cadet was being produced side by side with Chevrolet cars and trucks. The article went on to describe a tour of the works. Gearboxes and engines were tested on a Heeman-Highfield dynamometer: it is interesting to note that the engine and gearbox were initially run in on the dynamometer, tested under load, dismantled and eventually retested before being conveyed to another part of the building for assembly into a chassis. The article goes on to say that the front axle was drilled in one go and that the back axle was built up of steel components, and after the final drive had been assembled the complete unit was tested under load for noise and smooth running. The brakes were individually run in.

In another building gangs of men riveted chassis together, in addition to adding various parts such as springs, axles and brake gear. The chassis were then hoisted through an opening in the ceiling to a conveyor track on the floor above, where the engine-gearbox unit was bolted in place and coupled to the propellor shaft. Once the chassis was completed it was carried on the moving track into a paint booth where it was sprayed with black paint before entering a tunnel where the paint was dried. Upon leaving the tunnel, the chassis was fitted with road wheels and tyres. The next stage was the fitting of the body (complete with dashboard, instruments, floor, seats and all trim), which was lowered on to the chassis. The final operations were the fitting of the wiring loom, the lamps, rear wings and finally the radiator and bonnet. The vehicle was then thoroughly inspected and ready for delivery.

Depending on the speed of the track, each vehicle spent between two and two and a half hours being assembled. A vehicle came off the line every six minutes.

In the *Autocar* article of 1933 it states that at the time the proportion of Cadets and Bedford was about fifty-fifty. An interesting comment in the article concerns the demand for 6 volt electrics in export markets, saying that this was an area where there should be standardization.

Bodywork was well made. Vauxhall's bodies of this period were of composite construction whereby pressed steel panels were secured to wooden framework. Under the General Motors system the various parts of the framework were cut to standard sizes with the aid of jigs and special machines similar to those employed in making chassis components. After assembly each body received several coats of cellulose paint, which were dried in ovens through which the lines of bodies were carried automatically. Final inspection of the bodywork and paintwork was carried out under very bright lights in order to show any blemishes. The whole process achieved an excellent finish and consistency because of the close inspection at every stage of manufacture.

The 1930s have been referred to as the period of Vauxhall's engineering leadership. The reports in *The Motor* and *The Autocar* confirmed Vauxhall as a quality manufacturer and the GM Vauxhall re-established the reputation for reliability enjoyed by the marque in its earlier years.

*The Autocar* of 16 June 1933 introduced the new Light Six to an eager market. This model was known as the A type. Two engine sizes were offered, 12 hp ASY and 14 hp ASX, of which the 14 hp proved the more popular. Before the official launch the factory built up adequate stocks of the new model. On the launch day 250 Light Sixes were collected from the factory by Vauxhall dealers – an excellent piece of publicity masterminded by Sales Director A.F. Palmer Phillips. This was probably the first time a motor manufacturer had attempted this in the UK.

In addition to a choice of two horsepower ratings, two trim specifications were offered. The saloon cost £195; for £5 extra a sliding roof was specified. The De Luxe included a sliding roof in addition to 'no-draught' ventilation (quarter lights), chromium-plated lamps and flutes, folding centre arm rest, parcel nets and assist cards, all for £215. The very comprehensive specification included leather upholstery on the seats and on the door trim. The no-draught ventilating system was also introduced in America in 1933 on GM's cars. The A-type styling was similar to GM American models of 1933, as the basic shape had been introduced a year earlier by Harley Earl's famous studio. New for 1933 were the wing valances.

*The Autocar* road tested a 12/6 saloon for the 16 June 1933 edition. They praised the performance, brakes, comfort, gearchange, steering and turning circle. They noted that one shock absorber was not working correctly, but finished by saying, 'this is a car of which a good deal should be seen before long'. Although it should be borne in mind that road tests up to the 1960s were often written with the boardroom and advertising revenue in mind, there is no doubt that in the case of the A type Vauxhall had produced a superior Light Six. Sales took off very rapidly. The car gained an excellent reputation in the motor trade and with the private owner in the same way that the front wheel drive Cavalier and Astra have done in more recent times.

1933 sales of the Bedford commercial vehicles reached 16,000. Some of these sales were because of the van version of the A type, the 8 cwt ASYC (12 hp) and ASXC (14 hp) vans. This new van was the most refined in its class and offered excellent value for money; the 12 hp ASYC sold for £155 complete, which made it the cheapest six-cylinder van on the market. The van outlived the A-type car by several years, staying in production until 1939.

1934 was dominated by the introduction of the B-type Big Six car and the Bedford WT truck. There is no doubt that of the two the WT was the winner in terms of sales and profits for Vauxhall Motors. It had been shown at the Commercial Motor Show of October 1933, where it caused a sensation by virtue of the fact that, owing to its light unladen weight, it could legally travel at 30 mph. (Its influence was so strong that its basic design dominated British truck design for the next twenty years: it was Stepney Acre's masterpiece.) The new B type range had been introduced to the public at the 1933 motor show. The range consisted of the BY and BX, which were rated at 19.8 hp and 26.3 hp respectively, and the long wheelbase BXL which was also fitted with a larger engine.

The styling was pure 1934 GM, not dissimilar to the Chevrolet Master Series four-door Sedan. Following the trends of the time, the engine was moved forward in the chassis, thus increasing leg room for passengers, and the starter was operated by pressing the accelerator pedal. Immediately the engine fired, the starter switch was thrown out of engagement by vacuum created in the inlet manifold. A control unit was mounted on top of the starter motor, connected by a vacuum pipe to the inlet manifold. A small flush-fitting boot was another innovation.

Sales were slow at first but gradually picked up, although by the time production ceased in 1936 only 4,584 had been sold. This was fewer than the Cadet VY and VX at 5,932 and 3,759 respectively. The A type had a total production 1933–34 of 23,294.

It could be argued that the A-type range and the WT Bedford range were the most important models in Vauxhall's programme of the 1930s because of their tremendous sales success, thus repaying General Motors' faith in its new British plant. This sales success was reflected in the company's profits for 1936, £1.1 million. This was, apart from Morris, the best result of any British manufacturer for that year. The opposition were beginning to feel the winds of change at Luton. In fifteen months Vauxhall sold over double the number of cars in the 12/6 category, compared with Austin. Much of the competition lacked Vauxhall's design and flair. Although the B type could not be regarded as a sales success, in styling terms it echoed the A type's replacement the DX-DY range, which was unveiled at Olympia in the autumn of 1934 and would repeat the success of its predecessor, the A type, with 59,563 examples sold between 1935 and 1938.

Apart from the change in styling to a more modern shape, the D type introduced a number of important engineering changes. First among these was the use of Dubonnet independent front suspension. General Motors had introduced this system on Chevrolet and Pontiac for the 1935 model year. The original design was of French origin, made by Gustave Chedru. Chedru was financed by André Dubonnet of aperitif fame, who was also a racing driver. The A type and its predecessor the Cadet had good roadholding characteristics for the period. With the D type and subsequent models using variations of the Dubonnet suspension system, some of the roadholding qualities which had been praised in the A and Cadet models had been sacrificed in order to make 'all the roads of Britain feel like bowling greens'. Some makes in General Motors' American range received a superior short and long arm wishbone arrangement. With their new front suspension, Vauxhall had an important selling point which they demonstrated by various methods. It is interesting that Chevrolet continued to offer the option of a solid axle for those who preferred leaf springs at the front and in 1939 dropped the Dubonnet system completely, standardizing on the superior long arm/short arm arrangement. Of Vauxhall's competitors, Singer briefly used a bell crank independent front suspension system in mid-1934, with disastrous results. Hillman introduced a system in 1936, followed by Standard in 1939.

The aim of General Motors' designers in moving towards independent front suspension at this time was to obtain a very soft ride without consequent disadvantages of instability and inaccurate steering. With the Vauxhall the excessive pitching of some early American systems was absent. Under heavy braking, however, the front of the car would dip excessively. With the change to independent front suspension it was necessary to stiffen the chassis, which on the A type was not dissimilar to the earlier R type of the late '20s. This was achieved by adopting a cruciform braced design, sometimes referred to as an X frame, which replaced the previous design known as a ladder frame.

The new front suspension was 300 lb heavier. This additional weight was compensated for by raising the compression on the D-type engines from 5.5:1 to 6.25:1. In addition, a thermostat was placed in the cooling system and the engine was moved forward 4 in, thus bringing the rear seat within the car's wheelbase, which in turn afforded the rear passengers a better ride. As with the previous model, two engine sizes were offered, these being rated at 12 and 14 hp respectively. In terms of design the engines were little changed from the A series, with cubic capacities of 1530 cc and 1781 cc. As with the A and B types and the later G type the big ends were direct white metal lined. In the D type range changes were made to the gearbox: needle roller bearings replaced plain bearings in the mainshaft spigot and third speed gear, and a positive lock was introduced into the selector mechanism.

As with the A type there was a very wide range of coachbuilt bodies designed for the D-type chassis with factory approval. These ranged from the VC special by Abbot, which was based on the body of their Le Mans winning 4½-litre Lagonda style, to Martin Walter's four-door Wingham cabriolet, in addition to five factory approved drophead coupés, which ranged in price from £275 for the Grosvenor-built body to £298 for Tickford's four-light Jubilee.

Motoring magazines of the day were enthusiastic about the new range. It was noted that the handbrake position could be awkward for lady drivers, but very little comment was made about the handling of the car – although *The Motor* stated: 'If extra fast cornering is indulged in, some sway will arise.' Today it is recognized that while a D type is more pleasant to drive on an uneven surface such as a country lane, when it comes to a smooth surface such as an A road or motorway, its predecessor the A type suffers less from steering wander.

The pre-war family motorist was quite content to amble along at 30 to 40 mph. Certainly, speeds of

50 mph and 60 mph were considered to be fast. This was as much a result of narrow winding roads as of the design of the average British motor car, which by the end of the decade could be regarded, with the exception of Vauxhall and a few makes such as Lagonda which catered for the upper echelons of the market, as the most technically backward cars in Europe. As Laurence Pomeroy Junior later said, when quoting the Duke of Cambridge, and referring to successive generations of engineers employed by the likes of Austin and Morris, 'All change, at any time and for any purpose, is utterly to be deprecated.'

For some reason, in 1935 the 12 hp version outsold the 14 hp version by 70 per cent. In all other years of the D type's production, the 14 hp was the more popular.

The only changes for the 1936 season to the D type range was the availability of two-tone colour schemes. As in the previous year, wings were painted black. During the 1936 season the electric windscreen wipers were replaced by camshaft-driven units, thus relieving the battery and the dynamo. In recent times this system has been criticized in some circles, but today's commentators often forget that the electrical charging system of pre-war and immediate post-war years did not have the output of modern systems. In road tests the system was often commented upon favourably. The following year, 1937, saw a larger sump with a capacity of 9 pints. The worm and sector type steering box was replaced by a Burman-Douglas worm and nut design, and the camshaft was fitted with white metal bearings. Following the fashion of the time, easy-clean steel wheels replaced the original wire wheels and a new variation of the traditional Vauxhall grille appeared. In the new design the stoneguard was replaced by chromium-plated vertical bars which swept up into the bonnet line, giving what was known as a 'waterfall' grille. Complementing the new grille were new bonnet louvres, which consisted of five horizontal bars with four vertical arrows spaced between them. The changes gave the range a more modern appearance.

New for 1937 was the touring saloon, which was only available on the 14 hp chassis. At the rear was an opening steel trunk to which the spare wheel was bolted and housed in a pressed steel cover. The number of factory approved, coachbuilt bodies was reduced to four designs, from twenty only a few years earlier. These consisted of Whittingham and Mitchell's Stratford sports tourer, Martin Walter's Wingham cabriolet, and drophead coupés from Grosvenor and Tickford. During 1937 the arrow motifs were superseded on the bonnet louvres, production finally ceasing in 1938.

In the years leading up to the Second World War the pace of change quickened. By this time the Bedford range dominated the lightweight commercial vehicle market as well as the bus and coach market in the lightweight category (up to twenty-five seats) with their WTB model.

Even in its final year of production, the D-type range offered the best value and the best mechanical units in the 12/14 hp class, with prices starting from £195 for the 12 hp saloon. By comparison, Morris, Austin and Standard charged £225, £235 and £249 respectively.

The company was able to keep ahead of the competition because of the quality of staff employed in senior positions. From the middle of the decade new personnel joined the team. One of the first was David B. Jones ARCA, who joined Vauxhall in 1934 from the Royal College of Art. Originally his intentions had been to stay long enough to raise money for a holiday in France. In 1934 he was the Styling Department, where he was employed to model future designs suitable for production. He found he enjoyed the work and decided to stay. Eventually an assistant joined the new department, as it was a two-man job building the matrices for the full scale plaster models. By the early '70s Jones was in charge of 140 personnel in the styling department, part of the £2½ million Engineering and Styling Centre opened in 1964. In 1937 he had been joined by Tony Cooke from Rolls-Royce who was in charge of body design on cars and trucks. For many years the riding characteristics of Vauxhall and Bedford vehicles were frequently superior to their rivals'. In 1937 GM's suspension expert, Maurice Olley, was seconded to Vauxhall. He was of Welsh and Huguenot descent, being tall and distinguished, highly strung and with a subtle sense of humour. Olley started work at Rolls-Royce in 1912. Later he worked under the direct supervision of Frederick Royce at Le Canadel. When Rolls-Royce decided to build the Silver Ghost chassis for the US market at Springfield, Massachusetts, they found that the suspension was incompatible with American roads. Olley was Resident Engineer at Springfield, in charge of investigating the problem of wheel wobble or 'shimmy', but later became very involved with the problems of ride, handling and stability.

On one of his regular trips to Europe, Alfred Sloan had met André Dubonnet, and as a result of this meeting GM decided to adopt independent front suspension across the group's car range for the New York motor show of November 1933, as a direct result of Olley's experiments. The Dubonnet system was chosen for Chevrolet, Vauxhall, Opel and Pontiac.

Alex Taub was born into a Jewish working-class family employed in the fur trade in the East End of London. He was educated in the US as he had wealthy relations there. He had a cheerfully outrageous style of aggressiveness and his powers of persuasion were considerable. Short in stature, lean and dapper, he had the typical Jewish qualities of shrewdness and vitality; he was both optimistic and impatient! Taub regarded fuel economy as the prime objective, made a deep impression at Vauxhall and caused a considerable stir in the British motor industry.

The final new recruit for 1937 was Maurice Platt. Platt was already known to other members of the management team, in particular C.E. King and Charles Bartlett. Maurice Platt first met King in 1924 when visiting the firm for *The Motor* where he worked as a technical journalist, after receiving an engineering training. Later he became acquainted with Bartlett, who invited him to join the company in mid-1937. Platt worked with both Olley and Taub. On Taub's return to the States in late 1940, in order to enlist the interest of American engineers and manufacturers in the production of Frank Halford's Napier Sabre 2000 hp aero engine, which interestingly had single sleeve valves like Vauxhall's S type of the '20s. Alex Taub later recalled how, to his disillusionment, the Americans were interested only in picking up new ideas; no one was interested in making engines or components.

When Maurice Platt was put in charge of the Flat 12 Churchill tank engine there were still serious problems to be resolved. After the war he was responsible for the excellent range of engines fitted to the L and E types. In 1953 he succeeded King as chief engineer.

The first car to receive the new TT front suspension was the GY/GL range, introduced for the 1937 season at the London Motor Show in the autumn of the previous year. The new range was available in two wheelbases; the long variant was the GL. The engine was the well-proven 3215 cc unit which had been used in the 25 hp version of the previous B type range; it was also shared by the company's Bedford range. It endowed the GY with an 80 mph performance. With the G type Vauxhall returned to hydraulic brakes. This dual system was advanced for its day and was probably used because of P. Stepney Acre's distrust of hydraulic systems; his saying was, 'Where there is Lockheed there is trouble'. Initially a four-speed gearbox was used, replaced by a three-speed unit for the 1938 season. In both boxes the top two ratios had syncromesh.

The saloon (GY) had excellent performance and came fully equipped with fog lamp, reversing light, leather interior trim, sun roof and a heater for £315, with a yearly road tax of £18 15s. The new TT front suspension, together with leaf springs at the rear, was designed to give a good ride at the expense of good cornering at higher speeds. The G type was advertised at one time as the successor to the 30/98! However, with its rigid cruciform chassis, excellent brakes and good steering, it could have been the basis of a poor man's Bentley. What was needed was a suspension system more suited to a fast car and a nice four-light close-coupled sports saloon body.

The styling of the G type followed the general styling trends of the late '30s, with a waterfall radiator grille, easy clean wheels and a small boot. In addition to the saloon and limousine bodywork, some chassis were fitted with ambulance bodywork. A number of coachbuilt bodies from such firms as Grosvenor and Martin Walter were still available. As with previous models, the end result was in some cases a strikingly handsome car. Production of the G range finished in 1940, by which time some 6,822 had been sold. The G type was the last Vauxhall to have a chassis, apart from some export versions of the J type and the post-war L type.

In 1937 Vauxhall introduced the first modern small British car, the 10 hp H type, featuring a new 1204 cc four-cylinder engine with ohv and a three-bearing crankshaft, independent front suspension, hydraulic brakes and integral construction, with a fuel consumption of up to 40 mpg. The neat understated four-light body was, in the author's opinion, the nicest factory design since the A type saloon. Vauxhall spent £1 million developing the new design, which sold for £168 and £182 for the saloon de luxe. Again, the TT front suspension was used, offering a ride superior to Vauxhall's rivals.

With the H type's engine, Taub took a number of measures to maximize fuel economy. He recognized the importance of crank case ventilation, oil filtration and a quick warm up from a cold start in order to minimize the corrosion caused by acidic products of combustion. In addition to the normal thermostat in the cooling system, the engine also had a thermostatically controlled hot spot on the inlet manifold. With the co-operation of Zenith he redesigned the carburettor so the ratio of petrol and air delivered to the engine was weaker – that is, the proportion of petrol to air was reduced under part throttle conditions. In order to reduce the chance of misfiring, the spark plug gaps were widened and the polarity of the electrical system reversed. To further reduce the running costs, the engine was designed to burn lower octane petrol, then known as 'commercial' petrol. In order to prove the excellent fuel economy of the H type, many Vauxhall dealers were supplied with special test tanks and fitments. The dealers placed a car at the disposal of anyone who wished to test the fuel consumption of the Vauxhall 10. Many ordinary motorists obtained figures of 40 mpg, which was the figure Taub aimed at. The average for all press road tests was 43.9 mpg.

In January 1938, less than two months after the new car launch, an example was privately entered in the Monte Carlo rally by a team from Stourbridge. The car covered 2,275 miles without losing a single mark. It also achieved a good result in the final acceleration tests. The tool kit had not been used.

There were critics of the new car who tried to claim that independent suspension was not necessary for English roads; others said that independent front suspension would put up insurance rates because a bad accident would wreck such a car. A.F. Palmer-Phillips rebutted such nonsense in his usual direct way. Many of the critics were those in the motor trade, whose financial interest it was to sell other makes of 10 hp cars. Palmer-Phillips issued a leaflet entitled 'For the Information of the Motor Trade – the truth about the Vauxhall Ten'. The company had produced another winner; between 1937 and 1940 42,245 were produced. It is interesting to note that, like other manufacturers, Vauxhall Motors would test the opposition's products. Both Geoffrey King and Maurice Platt would refer to the day when Henry Crane, who by 1938 advised Sloan on engineering policy, decided to test a Morris 8 saloon. After a few miles he turned to Maurice and said, 'This is motoring in the raw! Let's go back to the plant.'

At the time of prototype testing prior to the launch of the new H type, work was in progress on companion saloon models which were to be ready by 1938. Six prototypes of the H type were produced; the majority of the initial design work, draughting and body testing was carried out by GM in the States.

At the same time as this activity was under way, the finishing touches were being put into place at the Vauxhall Engineering Research Building, which opened in 1938. The new building gave the company the best test and research facilities of any vehicle manufacturer in the UK. 1938 also saw the launch of I type 12/4 and the J type 14/6, these having many common parts. The I type (12 hp) and the J type (14 hp) were six-light designs. The 12 hp used an overboard 10 hp engine giving 1442 cc; 35 mpg was possible and the interior was roomier, thanks to a 7 in increase in wheelbase, from the H type's 94 in to 101 in. The 12 hp was 2 in wider than the 10 hp, and the 14 hp was 2 in wider than the 12 hp. The I type shared the same three-speed gearbox as the H type. Performance was reasonable. In all, some 10,164 examples were produced between 1938 and 1946, when the model was briefly re-introduced after the Second World War.

The 14/6 was well equipped with twin wipers, sliding roof, leather upholstery and adjustable steering column. The 1781 cc six-cylinder engine produced 48 bhp and the compression ratio was 6.75:1. Steering was still via a Busman-Douglas steering box. For the first time on a Vauxhall light six there were hydraulic brakes. As with the new H and I types, a three-speed gearbox was used; only on the J type was there the fairly unusual refinement of syncromesh on first gear. For export to Australia the body had the extra bracing of a chassis.

The J type turned the scales at 2,505 lb, some 200 lb lighter than some rivals. The result was excellent performance, with top speed around 70 mph and the ability to return 28–30 mpg.

Unlike its four-cylinder cousins, the J type had an external boot and a divided rear window. The new range also included a coupé, introduced in 1939 and styled by David Jones, and two vans; the 5/6 cwt HC introduced in the previous year and the 10/12 cwt JC.

Vauxhall Motors' performance during the years of the Second World War was no less impressive than its earlier exploits in the First World War. A number of cars were produced for the armed forces and government departments; however, the main production was of trucks, tanks and austerity buses. One very interesting activity at Vauxhall during the war years was the early development of Frank Whittle's jet engine. In 1940 Maurice Platt, together with King and Drew, visited Whittle and his staff at Lutterworth near Rugby. A second meeting was arranged at Luton, attended by Dr Roxbee Cox. Vauxhall contracted to provide design assistance to Whittle's company Power Jet Ltd, in addition to making various prototype parts. The Vauxhall design team was asked to study drawings with a view to suggesting modifications that would simplify some of the formidable production problems involved. When an engine had to be installed in an aircraft for flight testing, it was necessary to design the gearing to drive the accessories. The Vauxhall team was joined by John Brodie and Eric Moult who had worked with Frank Halford on the Napier Sabre engine. Later, Vauxhall and their De Havilland colleagues were asked by the Ministry if they would consider the design of an aircraft and a suitable engine. The end result was the Vampire and the Goblin jet engine.

At the beginning of 1941 it became obvious that all of Vauxhall's engineering expertise would be needed for the Churchill tank programme. In March of that year the Ministry of Aircraft Production awarded a direct contract to Rover to put into production Whittle's design. The results were disastrous, as described later in a book written by Frank Whittle.

Vauxhall's last involvement with Power Jets Ltd was to make a number of prototype parts, including the bladed rotor which was designed to deliver compressed air to the combustion chambers. The design called for extreme accuracy, being a casting of Elektron in which all surfaces had to be machined to complex geometrical requirements.

At the end of 1941 Ernest Hives of Rolls-Royce suggested to Spencer Wilks of Rover that Rover undertake the manufacture of the Rolls-Royce Meteor engine destined for the Cromwell tank, and that further development and eventual production of Whittle's jet engine should be undertaken at Rolls-Royce. This exchange of responsibilities was approved by the Ministry of Aircraft Production. Vauxhall's involvement in such products at this time illustrates the high regard in which the company was held. This was well illustrated in August 1948 when *The Autocar* described the new L-type range: 'Since it is well known that Vauxhall have one of the finest engineering development departments in the industry, the examination of their two designs becomes of particular technical interest. The Luton firm has on its staff some distinguished engineers.'

Had the war not intervened, Vauxhall had planed to replace the TT front suspension with a 'wishbone' system designed by Maurice Olley. In the event this did not appear until 1951.

Production of Vauxhalls recommenced in 1946. Initially the range consisted of the HIY type Ten-Four, I type Twelve-Four and the J type Fourteen-Six.

The stylish Hurlingham sports roadster was liked by *Motor Sport* when road tested.

The R type was replaced by the T type in 1930. These two examples, a Velox fabric saloon and the Kingston sportsman's coupé are, in the author's opinion, together with the Hurlingham, the best-looking Vauxhalls of the late Vintage period. The T type had forged connecting rods, a stiffer chassis and Luvax hydraulic shock absorbers. The T type was also known as the Silent 80 because it had silent third gear and the 3317 cc engine had a bore of 80 mm. The Hurlingham roadster had a top speed of 75 mph.

The Richmond saloon was a well-balanced design.

A handsome coupé on the T-type chassis. Notice the well-upholstered dickey seat. There were cast steps on the rear wing.

The T type was used on a number of official occasions. These two photographs show Prime Minister J. Ramsay Macdonald with his official car in 1931. Notice the period door mirror on the offside and the RAC badge. Macdonald is leaving Buckingham Palace after an audience with King George V. He was prime minister of the National Government, which was formed by members of all parties at the time of the depression that followed the Wall Street Crash..

A royal visit to Northampton, 17 November 1932. The cars are all 1932 T types and Cadets, identified by the dull chromium-plated stoneguards and larger hubs. The local dealer Grose placed a fleet of seven Vauxhalls at the disposal of the Royal party, when the Duke (later King George VI) and Duchess of York visited the town to open the New College of Technology and the John Greenwood Shipman Convalescent Home. The T types have Grosvenor Newmarket saloon bodies, first introduced at the Olympia Motor Show in October 1931.

The 'swan-neck' scuttle design of the Grosvenor Newmarket saloon is well illustrated in these two photographs. The smaller cars are Cadets.

A handsome 1932 two-seater drophead coupé on the Cadet chassis, with a body by Grose of Northampton, whose works can be seen on page 87 (bottom).

An example of a 1931 Cadet saloon with the factory body and leather trim for the interior. From 1932 the Cadet had a syncromesh gearbox.

The very popular A type, Vauxhall's first real volume seller. Prices were from £195 for the standard saloon which didn't have quarter lights, sunshine roof or chromium-plated flute. The deluxe saloon is shown. The 12 hp (ASY type) and the 14 hp (ASX type) were the best in their class at the time.

A 1934 ASY 12 hp de luxe shown in 1965. The saloons were never two tones as shown here, although the very rare coupé model was. The wheels were painted in a contrasting colour which matched the interior. A popular combination was black coachwork with green leather interior and matching green wheels.

This neat little tourer with coachbuilt body was actually a police car. Many stylish coachbuilt bodies were available on the A-type chassis.

The 20 hp Vauxhall Big Six BY type, introduced in late 1933. In the same year the *Vauxhall Motorist* magazine was introduced, price 2*d*. In 1935 a larger format version was launched and sold in W.H. Smith's for 4*d*.

As with the smaller A types, examples of the BY (20 hp), BX (26 hp) and BXL (26 hp long wheelbase) were fitted with various types of coachbuilt body. This example shows the then Duke of Kent riding in a 1935 Wingham tourer, which had a Martin Walter body.

Two photographs of a Grosvenor-bodied BXL of 1934 vintage. Ideal transport for Mr Mayor!

A BY or BX tourer with the then Duke of Gloucester at Cootamundra, New South Wales. His escorts are men of the New South Wales Light Horse.

Air race heroes C.W.A. Scott and T. Campbell-Black shown leaving Victoria Station, London on the evening of 14 December 1934. They were the winners of the England–Australia International Air Race of 1934, covering the distance between Mildenhall and Melbourne in 70 hours 54 minutes in a specially designed De Havilland Comet DH 88. The car is a BY or a BX tourer with a Martin Walter Wingham body.

A 1936 DY fitted with the Martin Walter Wingham body designed for the DY and DX range. This 12 hp car cost £325 new and was restored by its owner John Mullen, who for many years was editor of the excellent *Flute News*, the newsletter of the Vauxhall Owners' Club.

On 28 October 1936 the then Duke of Kent came to Luton to open the new Town Hall and visit Vauxhall Motors. Here he is seen arriving in a 1937 model Vauxhall 25 hp (GL type) to tour the factory. The car's body is by Grosvenor.

A well-restored DX (14 hp) of 1936. The DY (12 hp) and the DX continued the sales success of the A type.

Some more restored Vauxhalls of the late 1930s, belonging to members of the Vauxhall Owners' Club. From the left, a 1938 DY, 1939 H type 10 hp and a 1937 DY. The club covers all types of Vauxhall from 1903 to 1957.

The H type was the first modern small British car. The design was neat and stylish; David Jones at his best. This 1938 restored example is finished in the original silver grey colour.

A GL, with limousine body by Grosvenor, offered its passengers comfort with good performance for its time, although lacking the elegance of Grosvenor's coachwork from the beginning of the decade.

The factory body on a GL chassis of around 1938 vintage, with an 80 mph performance and dual circuit brakes. The car's full potential was let down by its TT front suspension.

The H type was very popular in export markets. Shown here is one such car having the wheels removed before being placed in a wooden crate.

Vauxhalls and Bedfords were sold all around the world except in North America. Bedford's slogan 'you see them everywhere' had the merit of being true, as can be seen from this photograph.

The fluid lines of the J type shown to advantage. Introduced in 1939 at £230 the 14 hp J type had hydraulic brakes and 70 mph performance, combined with nearly 30 mpg. Production ceased in 1940 because of the war effort. Between 1939 and 1940 Vauxhall Motors sold 14,698 J types. Some examples went to the Royal Air Force.

# 1941–1960: FOURS AND SIXES

Although the commercial and military vehicles produced by Vauxhall are not within the scope of this book, it is worth pointing out that Vauxhall Motors' record in the Second World War was a very fine one. The production of Vauxhall cars and civilian-type Bedfords continued for a few months after 3 September 1939; many were built for war-related use. However, before long only military vehicles were being produced. On Friday 30 August, at 4.50 p.m., the factory took a direct hit from German bombers. Sadly, one woman and thirty-eight men were killed; because no machine tools were damaged, within a few days production was back to about a thousand vehicles a week. Vauxhall's total wartime output of vehicles was approximately 250,000, and they also supplied parts to the value of £18,450,156 between 1939 and 1945. From July 1941 the famous Churchill tank went into production. In the same year the government authorized Vauxhall to produce a small number of commercial vehicles for civilian use, and in 1942 the well-known OWB bus chassis went into production.

In 1944 Vauxhall had produced a booklet which was circulated throughout the motor industry, attacking the graduated annual Treasury tax based on rated horsepower. In the booklet Sir Charles Bartlett (knighted in 1945) stated: 'Were it not for this tax on units of horsepower, car manufacturers would list fewer models and produce each one more cheaply than at present. Suppliers of components would benefit and engineering departments would no longer have to spead their resources over a wide variety of products.' The SMMT had put forward the idea of taxation based on engine size. Bartlett, however, was of the opinion that a flat rate of tax should be established for the majority of cars used in the United Kingdom. In 1946 a tax based on engine size was imposed, but in the Budget of 1947 this was replaced by a flat rate, irrespective of engine size. As a result of these changes Vauxhall stopped production of the 10 hp engine; the I type was taken out of production, as was the post-war HIY Ten. Using the four-light from the Ten fitted with a 1442 cc engine taken from the I-type Twelve-Four and a slightly higher rear axle ratio, the company produced what they called the HIX Twelve-Four. As with the I type, horizontal bars replaced vertical bars on the grille.

The post-war J type was still the best performer in its class. The styling department changed the design of the bonnet louvres and the faces of the instruments.

Originally Vauxhall had intended to produce a modified HIX body and a modified J body for the new range announced in August 1948. However, Edward Riley, who had succeeded J.D. Mooney in 1941 and was elected Vice-President of GM in 1942, objected, insisting that one model was adequate until new buildings, new machine tools and larger presses were available. Bartlett held his ground. A meeting was organized, and Ormond Hunt, who had designed the Chevrolet 'Cast-Iron Wonder' back in the '20s and had now been promoted to Executive Vice-President, suggested the way forward was to transplant the six-cylinder engine for the J type's replacement into the modernized four-light HIX body.

The new engine was an updated and modified version of the 14 hp unit. Now displacing 2275 cc, it would have been rated at 18 hp under the old system. The new design introduced in August offered the lively six-cylinder Velox and also the frugal Wyvern. Even with a relatively high back axle ratio of 4.125:1 the 55 bhp Velox had what the Vauxhall advertising manager described as 'Flashing acceleration and effortless cruising at mile-a-minute speeds'. This was partly true until one tried to use the available performance on a twisting country road; then the limitations of the TT suspension became all too obvious. Had the car been fitted with the later 'wishbone' front suspension, the more enthusiastic motorist could have enjoyed roadholding more in keeping with the once-hallowed name of Velox.

In redesigning the six-cylinder engine emphasis had been placed on a flat torque curve. In this Maurice Platt and his team were successful. The engine gave over 100 lb from 800 to 2,500 rpm, reaching its maximum of 106 lb at 1200 rpm. Such figures endowed the new Velox with an excellent top gear performance. The engine, the last longstroke design from Luton, was a first class design, enabling the Velox to reach a top speed of 75 mph. By today's standards the acceleration was slow, with 0–30 in 7.4 seconds, 0–50 in 19.3 seconds and 0–60 in 30.6 seconds: these figures were inferior to the Standard Vanguard (Phase 1 and 2), the Morris Six (Series MSO) and the Austin A70 Hereford.

The Wyvern had a top speed of around 62 mph, which was the slowest in its class. In terms of acceleration it was bottom of the league, with 0–30 in 9.9 seconds and 0–50 in 27.8 seconds. The 0–60 figure wasn't quoted because of the car's low top speed. In terms of fuel consumption both models gave good results, with 25–28 mpg being feasible with the Velox and around 33–35 mpg with the Wyvern. With the Velox, Vauxhall used a pressurized cooling system for the first time, operating at 4 lb, thus raising boiling point to 223°F at sea level.

Another first for Vauxhall was the use of a column gear change, following the trends of the time. The gear change was better than that of many rivals who adopted this idea, but the Velox lost the syncromesh first gear used on the J type.

The cars were well finished, the Velox having hide-covered seats. Metallichrome colours of blue, grey, green and (for the Velox only) fawn were available.

In service the cars proved reliable and economical to run, although the TT front suspension could give trouble on uneven road surfaces, such as those in Africa. In the TT suspension system the torsion bar and tube were extremely highly stressed. Both Vauxhall's production engineers and the steel manufacturers had real problems in maintaining the very high standards required to avoid fatigue failures. Mechanics at Vauxhall dealers didn't always understand the subtleties of adjusting the ride height and thus troubles ensued. Despite being an ingenious design, the TT front suspension did not perform well in the hostile environment in which motor cars operate.

Maurice Olley introduced to Vauxhall Motors procedures which enable engineers to measure the overall stiffness of integral steel bodies, in addition to bodies bolted to a chassis frame. Such experiments gave factual data to body designers which they had not had previously. They started a trend at Vauxhall towards structural analysis which, over the coming years, became increasingly scientific and mathematical. He also introduced to Vauxhall simple experimental methods for the investigation of suspension and handling problems.

The LIP-type Velox and LIX Wyvern were ideal cars for what were austere times. Harold Drew, C.E. King's assistant, was partly responsible for the understated design.

One of the features of life at Vauxhall under managing director Charles Bartlett was the monthly meeting of the product committee. The committee was there to formulate product policy, in addition to discussing, approving or dismissing proposed changes to the specification and design of cars and trucks that were beyond the jurisdiction of the engineering department. The meetings were chaired by Bartlett; King and Drew represented engineering; costings were dealt with by Bill Laskey, the firm's supply manager; production was the province of factory manager Reg Pearson; and finally A.F. Palmer-Phillips covered sales and service.

Palmer-Phillips was often thinking of ways to promote the specification of Vauxhall cars and Bedford trucks which in his opinion would make them more attractive to the potential purchaser. In this he was very often frustrated by Bartlett, who was extremely cost conscious, as was Laskey. Drew was almost always sceptical of new ideas, being very much the realist. He knew that useless frills adversely affected productivity.

At times the committee members would meet in David Jones' styling studio to discuss new colours or trim materials, as well as changes to the outward appearance of Vauxhall cars and Bedford trucks. Despite disagreements at senior level prior to their launch, the L range sold well with sales figures between 1948 and 1951 of 55,409 and 76,919 for the Wyvern and Velox respectively.

The L type was not only popular in the UK but also in export markets. At this time it was extremely difficult to obtain a new car in Britain; in fact, the London Motor Show was nicknamed the 'Export only Show'. One reason for the success of the new Vauxhalls in export markets was that they would start easily, whatever the temperature or climate. This was owing to the standards laid down by Alex Taub before his return to America. The products of many British motor vehicle manufacturers at this time, while performing well on good roads at home, encountered problems overseas where such easy conditions did not always exist. This resulted in a gradual loss of reputation with the overseas customer.

Vauxhall's stylist David Jones was an ardent admirer of Harley Earl designs. Jones was responsible to the Vauxhall management, as were all divisional executives at Luton. However, his admiration for Earl's work meant that Luton's styling tended to be in line with GM's trends in America. This occasionally proved to be a mixed blessing.

A number of American and British motor vehicle manufacturers had the opportunity in the late '40s to take over the Volkswagen design. All senior personnel, whether in Detroit, Luton or Coventry turned down this chance, considering the car crude and unrefined. In the GM camp there was only one supporter, William Swallow, who in later years was Chairman of Vauxhall Motors and knighted for his services to industry.

For eleven years Swallow was a design engineer with the Pressed Steel Co. at Oxford, working under Dr George Kelley of the Budd company on integral bodies for the Rootes Group and Morris Motors. In January 1947 Swallow joined GMOO (General Motors Overseas Organization) in New York. At this time Edward Riley was looking into the possibility of producing an austerity car for under-developed countries (not to be confused with the Holden project). The idea was that such a car could be constructed of parts taken from the various car divisions within General Motors. Swallow put forward the idea that the VW would make an ideal basis for an industry car, rather than assembling a vehicle from American parts. It has been said that Swallow nearly lost his job at GMOO for going against the consensus of opinion at the time, which was that the VW wouldn't last for more than a few years. How wrong they were!

Throughout 1948 to 1950 work was under way for the designing and launching of the company's first all new post-war models. In addition there were plans for increasing the floor area at Luton by 30 per cent. It was therefore necessary to invest heavily in new plant and machinery and in the tooling relating to new models. With the company's expansion in mind, it was decided to create two new posts: a director of forward planning with a seat on the board and a production engineering manager. These positions were filled by Walter Hill and Harold Johnson. Although both men were new to Vauxhall, they were both GM trained. English-born Walter Hill had worked for GMOO in Detroit, Australia and New Zealand. He had earned a reputation for working amicably with different types of people. Harold Johnson had worked for Cadillac in his earlier years. By 1936 he was master mechanic, or in modern terms director of manufacturing. In 1946 he was directing a research group developing new techniques in the manufacture of vehicles. Johnson was remembered by those who knew him as very American, finding England strange at first and yet only a few years later trying in vain to dissuade Edward Riley from sending him back to Detroit.

In 1919 a young man, Reg Pearson, joined Vauxhall Motors, operating a lathe in the machine shop. Like Charles Bartlett he proved to be very good at labour relations and to possess a good deal of common sense. By the time preparations for the new E type were under way, Pearson was a member of the board. He later received the OBE and was knighted. By this time Pearson was in charge of all manufacturing in addition to the tooling and inspection departments.

As the programme for the new E type accelerated towards the launch date, some members of the product committee, including Charles Bartlett, wondered if they had made the correct decision in going for a one-body programme with a design that was quite a bit heavier, in addition to having larger overall dimensions. There were some members who considered continuing the existing L-type Wyvern and producing the new body only in six-cylinder Velox style.

In the spring of 1950 Harold Drew returned to London from America, where he had been convalescing at Edward Riley's residence in Buck's County, Pennsylvania after a serious operation in the previous year. Since neither Drew nor Riley was in favour of complicated car programmes at this stage of Vauxhall's development, partly because of the time and effort needed to develop the commercially important Bedford programme, common sense prevailed and the E-type programme went ahead as originally planned.

In November 1950 Drew became chief engineer and C.E. King, then aged sixty, was promoted to director of engineering. At the end of that year Walter Hill became chairman of General Motors Ltd at Hendon and was responsible for the activities of AC Sphinx, Delco-Remy and Frigidaire; he retained his seat on the Vauxhall board and continued to show an interest in Luton.

Britain's other American-owned manufacturer, Ford, introduced a modern range of cars – the Zephyr Six and the Consul – at the 1950 Motor Show. Up to this date the Ford car range had maintained a reputation for robust design but mechanically they were basically early '30s designs which were becoming increasingly outdated in the post-war world. With their new 1.5-litre Consul and 2.3-litre Zephyr Six, Ford offered very serious competition, not only to Vauxhall but also to the rest of the British motor industry. Vauxhall's response came in the autumn of the following year, 1951, with the launch of the new Wyvern and Velox (types EIP and EIPV). The £14 million expansion programme of 1948 was showing results, with a new 19½ acre building opened the previous year.

The new E type was wider than the Consul and Zephyr Six. The existing 2¼-litre and 1½-litre engines from the L type were initially used. Vauxhall was by now expert in lightweight integral body design; the new designs were lighter than those of their rivals. The reception given to the new range by the public, the press and dealers was very enthusiastic, which was not surprising considering the offerings from Austin, Morris, Hillman and Standard. At last Vauxhall had a modern wishbone front suspension system. Early cars had a side opening bonnet which could be easily removed for total accessibility. This system had also been used by Buick. In terms of styling the overall shape was typical GM of the period, first introduced in 1948 on the Cadillac Series 61 and the Oldsmobile Futuramic.

In April 1952 new short-stroke engines were introduced, more in keeping with the E type's modern design. The new engines were of 1508 cc and 2262 cc, sharing a bore and stroke of 79.3 x 76.2 mm. The Wyvern could at last reach 70 mph. It was still noted for its excellent economy, which was the best in the six-seater class, returning over 30 mpg on a run. At £771 it was very competitively priced. The new six-cylinder Velox engine produced 65 bhp, 20 hp more than the four-cylinder Wyvern. Thanks to the flat torque curve and 108 lb of torque at 1200 rpm, the re-engined Velox restored Vauxhall's reputation for lively six-cylinder cars: 60 mph could now be reached in 20 seconds, with a top speed of 80 mph. With the new wishbone front suspension, handling was much improved compared with previous models fitted with the TT front suspension. The ride was still the best in its class and the Burman recirculating ball steering box ensured light steering. It was possible to make the Velox into a rapid smooth-handling car by tuning the engine and suspension. V.W. Derrington of Kingston on Thames, Surrey, offered a three SU carburettor conversion for the Velox. By polishing the ports and combustion chambers and raising the compression ratio the Velox engine could be persuaded to produce around 100 bhp. Vauxhall's C.E. King had a tuned Velox built at the factory. Geoffrey King would recall how this car would out-accelerate other cars of the day and had a 100 mph performance. The engine was blueprinted and tuned at Vauxhall Motors and the suspension modified to accept the car's much higher performance. It is a pity that General Motors showed no interest in motor sport at this time; a factory competition department could have enhanced the car's image. There were, however, a number of private entries in international rallies. In 1955 a Velox was placed seventh in the popular East African Safari Rally.

At one stage of the production, the Velox was the cheapest six-cylinder six-seater car in Britain, priced at £833.

Vauxhall continued its policy of gradual development throughout the E type's production. 1952 saw a new facia design introduced while a conventional bonnet was introduced in April 1953. In the following year the Cresta was introduced in addition. This was in effect a de luxe version of the Velox. It was introduced in October 1954, and undercut Ford's Zephyr Zodiac by £7, retailing at £844 including purchase tax. The Cresta featured two-tone colour schemes which suited the car extremely well. The two-tone effect was carried through to the interior, which featured leather bench seats, an improved facia suitable for either right- or left-hand drive models and a heater as standard equipment.

Styling changes do not always mean styling improvements! In 1955, though, all the E type range received a new concave die-cast grille, which together with a slightly lower bonnet line improved the appearance of the range. Re-designed bumpers which incorporated over-riders also helped the car's appearance. One of the most popular colour combinations (which particularly suited the Cresta) was maroon and cream, not unlike the colours used by British Railways on the coaches of express trains at this time. Other changes for the much improved E type were spats for the rear wheels, an improved gearshift linkage, flashing indicators in place of trafficators, flexible coupling between steering box and steering column, increased diameter for the petrol filler pipe and finally chromium-plated top piston rings. The end result was a good-looking car, in particular the Cresta.

On the personnel front, Harold Drew was appointed to the position of chief engineer for GMOO in Detroit in spring 1953. His position at Vauxhall was then filled by Maurice Platt.

Early in 1954 Platt and Jones visited Edward Riley in New York to discuss with Riley and his planning staff a product programme, in line with Vauxhall's future expansion, which had recently been approved in principle by the Oversea Policy Group in Detroit. Vauxhall Motors Ltd had done well in 1953, its Jubilee Year, producing 110,000 vehicles, of which 66,000 were exported. The company's best overseas markets were Australia, New Zealand, South Africa, Belgium, Denmark and Sweden. It was agreed that it was essential to rid Vauxhall of the production limitations that had resulted in Riley insisting on a programme of one basic body with two optional engines in the preceding post-war years. In view of the GM plans, which were already under way, to further enlarge Vauxhall's car and truck facilities, Riley agreed to go ahead with a two-model programme in which there would be a considerable difference in size, performance and price of new four- and six-cylinder cars. Riley put forward a production date of autumn 1957 for the smaller car and suggested that the larger car, which would replace the E-type Velox and Cresta, could come into production six or twelve months later.

In 1954 work had started on a new car production building at Luton and the transfer of Bedford trucks to Dunstable. The cost of this investment was £36 million.

For the final two years of the E type production, modification continued on the existing designs. On the 1956 models the windscreen and rear window apertures were increased in size by 12 per cent and 60 per cent respectively. Proper window winding mechanisms replaced the previous design, in which the side windows were regulated by pulling up or pushing down a small piece of perspex attached to the top of the glass. Vinyl headlining was introduced for the 1956 model year, and also a larger rear mirror. The Wyvern and Velox received what was claimed to be improved vinyl seat trim, while the Velox and Cresta models were fitted with arm rests which also served as door pulls. A new grille, which although still of concave design, was pressed rather than diecast, giving the front end a less expensive appearance. Cresta models received a chromium moulding along the flanks. For 1956 the darker colour was applied to the roof and flanks below the chrome moulding.

Up to this time Vauxhall's integrally constructed cars were prone, like other early examples of this type of construction, to rust and body corrosion. In an effort to eradicate this one fault, a thicker coat of paint was used on bodywork for the 1956 models. It would be a few years until matters improved in this area and it would remain a weak point in Vauxhall car design until the 1960s.

Up to the 1956 models, the E type was prone to early locking of the rear wheels under heavy braking, which could result in a skid. In an effort to cure this tendency, Vauxhall engineers altered the system so that the braking effort on the rear wheels was reduced in proportion to the front; now the proportion was 64 per cent front, 36 per cent rear as against a previous 59 per cent and 41 per cent. Mechanics in Vauxhall dealers were doubtless pleased that at last the rear brake drums were cast separately from the hubs; no longer did they have to use a puller to remove rear drums.

When the 1957 models were displayed at the Earls Court Motor Show in London in October 1956, further changes in the vehicle had taken place. After over twenty years the cam-shaft driven wipers were replaced: for the first time since the demise of the A-type Light Six, Vauxhall Motors fitted electrically powered wipers on their cars. Also, compression ratios were raised to 6.8:1 on the Wyvern and 7.7:1 on the Velox, and the carburettor was changed from a Zenith 30 VIG 7 to a 34 VN. The styling modifications consisted of chromium-plated horizontal bars for the grille and new chromium moulding along the flanks, which on the Cresta model contrasted with the second colour.

The E type sold very well, some 344,386 examples leaving the factory between the autumn of 1951 and the end of 1956. Sales of the Wyvern finished during spring 1957, with production of the Velox finishing during the summer of the same year. Looking back forty years after production finished, it is plain to see that, together with their rivals from Ford, the Vauxhall Wyvern and Velox offered families of the time stylish yet roomy transport with above average ride and extremely tough mechanicals. Both Hillman and the four-cylinder Morris had gutless side valve engines until, in the case of Hillman, 1954. The ohc Morris Six suffered from lack of water capacity around the bores, poor steering, expensive engine maintainance and handling not much better than an L type! The majority of Austins of the period had dreadful handling, poor steering and an awful column gear change.

The new smaller four-cylinder car was the F type, the first of the Victor series. Edward Riley had suggested a weight target of 1900 lb, which was 500 lb lighter than the Wyvern and even slightly lighter than the then current Opel Rekord two-door saloon. David Jones and his team produced two different designs, one which was typical mid-'50s Americana and another which was said to be simple in line but unfortunately was not particularly good looking either. By the time the realistic full size styling 'clays' were produced, Harlow H. Curtice was president of General Motors. Curtice was a man known for on-the-spot decisions. His plan to visit GM European plants in

1954 included a trip to Vauxhall. This was the time of the panoramic windscreen in America and it was decided that all GM divisions would use it, followed by the overseas divisions. All US manufacturers had to comply; even Packard, known hitherto for the understated appearance of its cars, was forced to change to the new style for the 1955 models. David Jones' American-looking clay representation of the new F type therefore featured a panoramic windscreen, along with other styling details in line with Harley Earl's styles of the time.

On his visit to Luton, Curtice examined both designs but the end result was in no doubt. Curtice took the view that Vauxhall would gain a real lead by being the first manufacturer in Europe to put a car with a panoramic windscreen into mass production, and despite counter arguments from some engineers he held to his opinion that the sales advantages were such that there was no other option.

Curtice decided to put some of the design work of the new model in the hands of Fisher Body in Detroit, first suggesting some detail changes. (Fisher had been purchased by GM in 1926.) The reason for the work sharing was the short lead time to production. The new PA-type six-cylinder Velox and Cresta models, the design of which was entirely 'in house' at Vauxhall Motors, were due to enter production by autumn 1957. This required the employment of extra staff as time was at a premium. Luckily for Vauxhall and Curtice, Fisher Body had time to devote to the new F type owing to a lull in the American programme. Vauxhall engineering staff received help in planning preparation from Pete Hoglund, who came to Luton from Opel. For a number of years Hoglund was Riley's second in command; he was well liked and noted for being very level-headed.

In addition to preparing the two new cars for production, Vauxhall Motors was in the process of testing the first Bedford diesel engines, due for production in 1957, and improved models in the Bedford range. Between the start of the Victor and the launch of the car, engineering and styling staff increased by 60 per cent. On 14 December 1954 the co-operative plan for the F type was launched.

In the spring of 1955 Walter Hill stood down, being replaced by Philip Copelin from GM Continental at Antwerp.

As the Victor programme gained momentum, some Vauxhall engineers went to work in Detroit on the project. The first prototype ran on 13 October 1955. With work progressing at full speed on the new Victor model, David Jones and his team had been very busy designing the body for the new PA type. On 14 October Harlow Curtice paid his second visit to Vauxhall Motors, this time to view the styling model that Jones had prepared. Curtice declared the new design a winner and announced that the production date for the Victor would be pushed forward to the spring of '57. By March 1956 Maurice Platt had examined the Victor prototype, now stripped down after completing a night and day 25,000 mile test for durability. Apart from sealing problems around the doors, the new design had stood up very well to this rigorous exercise – and Fisher engineers were able to design a new seal to overcome the one apparent problem.

The Victor production line started on 1 February 1957, and in March the Victor was on display at the Geneva Motor Show, where it was well received; in fact it eventually became Britain's leading export model. In the home market views were mixed regarding the Victor's styling; however, praise was accorded to the model's excellent handling, stability and roadholding. Priced at £728, the vehicle was powered by an improved version of the engine seen in the 1957 Wyvern, now developing 55 bhp.

Although the cubic capacity was still 1508 cc, considerable work had been carried out with a view to making the unit stronger. The new cylinder block was deeper and the cylinder head was now held in place by studs of equal length. Larger inlet valves and separate inlet ports helped efficiency. Syncromesh reappeared on first gear of the three-speed gearbox, with column change for the first time since the end of production of the J type in 1947. Overall gearing was 16.3 mph at 1000 rpm. For the first time on a Vauxhall the clutch was hydraulically operated. As with previous models, the hydraulic brakes were of Lockheed design and manufacture. One change from the E type was the use of twin front wheel cylinders; 8 in drums were used all round, giving the 20 cwt saloon good braking properties.

The top speed was around 75 mph with 60 coming up in 25 seconds, which together with a fuel consumption of around 32–35 mpg all helped the car's popularity. Early models encountered problems with the synthetic door seals, despite the redesign. It was also found that there were problems holding the clearances around the doors at the required specifications, owing to complex curvatures of the body. With more robust seals the problem was overcome. Compared with the nightmare problems that BMC encountered with their front wheel drive designs, or Rootes with the Hillman Imp, it was a very small problem, although at the time, as anyone who has ever worked in the service department of a motor manufacturer will know, it never seems that way!

In the following spring a handsome estate car version of the Victor was introduced. This was the company's first in-house design, previous efforts being conversions of saloons by companies such as Martin Walter.

The new range was now complete with two models. In addition to the basic saloon there was the Super, which offered extra refinements such as armrests on all doors, two-tone horn, extra bright trim, exhaust tail pipe outlet through the off side of the bumper and a rear ashtray.

The Victor stayed in production until 1961. In the intervening period there were a number of changes to the external styling as well as interior trim. The first of these was replacing the tail pipe on the Super so that it terminated underneath the bumper. In September 1958 the first significant changes to the original design appeared with the Series II. More conventional bumpers replaced the earlier type, stainless steel trim was no longer applied to the side window frames and central pillar and the crease was deleted from the rear doors. There was now only one crease in the bonnet instead of the original two. An additional model was added to the range, the de luxe, which had leather-covered seats, those at the front being individual seats as opposed to bench seat used on other models. In August 1960 the final version of the F type appeared. The most noticeable differences lay in the deeper rear window, redesigned facia and horizontal chrome-plated bars on the grille.

The total number of F types produced was 330,000. The basic mechanical units were very reliable, and the original 1957 Series F type is today highly collectable, as are most old Vauxhalls. The estate car version is now particularly rare in the UK.

Of all motor cars designed and produced in Britain during the 1950s, one of the best looking was Vauxhall's PA range. It could be argued that the PA was the most attractive of all GM designs of the period apart from the Chevrolet Corvette. The series 1 and 2 PA were probably David Jones' finest designs.

Unlike the Victor, the early PAs did not suffer from water leakage around the door shuts. Vauxhall engineers had modified the door seals before production began.

When announced to the public in the autumn of 1957, priced at £983 and £1,073 – excellent value for money – the new Cresta and Velox made the opposition look suddenly old-fashioned! The new cars gave an appearance of being long and low. In fact the PA Velox and Cresta were 5 in longer and 2 in wider than the previous E types, in addition to being 4½ in lower. There was also an increase in weight compared with the E type. The Velox and Cresta now turned the scales at 22¾ cwt, compared with 22.1 cwt for the E type Velox/Cresta. The overall gearing was reduced slightly from 18.4 mph at 1000 rpm to 17.5 mph at 1000 rpm. A top speed of around 90 mph, together with excellent handling and good brakes and a fuel consumption of 22/23 mpg, made these cars formidable competition for others in the class.

As with the Victor, the flutes were now along the sides of the body. All panels, apart from the doors, bootlid and bonnet were stress-bearing. The differences between the two models were confined to external chromium-plated trim and interior appointments. The Velox came with twin sun visors, two-speed electric wipers, armrests on all doors, twin horns and a folding centre arm rest for the rear seat. Dual tone paint, white wall tyres and full wheel trims identified the Cresta. The interior featured an electric clock, the choice of leather, rayon or elastofab (all in two contrasting colours) for the seat facings, chrome-plated horn ring and door trims in two colours to match the seats.

The 2.3-litre six-cylinder engine featured an improved design of Zenith carburettor but in other respects was identical to the unit used in the final four months of production of the six-cylinder E type. 76 bhp was produced at 4400 rpm with 124 lb ft torque at 1800 rpm making for relaxed top gear motoring.

The front suspension consisted of wishbones, coil springs and an anti-roll bar. The rear leaf springs had a slight reverse camber. The brakes were of Lockheed manufacture and, like the Victor, the clutch was hydraulically operated. Heavier gauge steel for the bonnet, larger quarter lights and a centre armrest for the front seat on the Cresta were some of the improvements introduced towards the end of 1958. In May of the following year an estate car conversion by Friary Motors of Basingstoke was offered. The cost was £1,222 for the Velox version and £1,308 for the Cresta.

In August 1959 further changes took place to the PA range, with a handsome new radiator grille and one-piece rear window being the most noticeable. Rear passengers gained in extra legroom, the seats were redesigned for improved comfort and there was an improved heater design for the Cresta.

Improvements to the engine resulted in an increase in capacity to 2651 cc, a rise in bhp to 95 at 4600 rpm and a change in the rear axle ratio, plus the fitting of 14 in wheels. The beautiful oval tail lights of the earlier models were replaced with a less attractive design. The tail fins were slightly larger and this was emphasized by running the contrasting colour along the fin which terminated in a V motif. Further changes which detracted from the original design were a fake wood effect on the facia and door cappings, and a new speedometer which was of the revolving drum type, changing colour from green to orange at 30 mph and to red from 60 mph. Genuine improvements were new 10 in front brake drums, the option of Laycock de-Normanville overdrive at £64, GM Hydramatic automatic transmission for an extra £170 and from the autumn of 1961 disc brakes were an option, as were individual front seats. In March 1962 the Vauxhall warranty was extended from six to twelve months. In all, some 173,759 examples were produced, of which 100,847 were exported. The type identification letters are: Velox PAS: October 1957 to August 1960; Velox PADY: August 1960 to October 1962; Cresta PAD: October 1957 to August 1960; Cresta PADX: August 1960 to October 1962.

Vauxhall had done well in the 1950s. By 1956 their profit per vehicle was £80, which was the best in the British motor industry. Premature rusting of bodywork was a problem which would be gradually overcome in the 1960s. The extraordinary popularity of the Bedford chassis would continue into the next decade. The company's most popular truck, the TK, was launched at the 1960 Commercial Motor Show to all-round applause. 1961 saw the introduction of the handsome FB Victor. This new design had been developed over the previous two years.

Owing to the Second World War production of Vauxhall cars ceased after 1940 so that the factory could devote its efforts to military production. Here we see Winston Churchill on a tour of Bristol and South Wales, raising his famous 'John Bull' hat in recognition of the cheers of the crowd in a war-damaged Bristol street. The car is a B-type tourer from the mid-1930s. Notice the white painted bumpers and the mask on the off side headlight.

In the late 1940s Clement Attlee's Labour Government believed in exporting British goods to recoup some of the millions paid to America for war materials under their lease lend scheme. The British motorist found that cars for the home market were in very short supply and as a result pre-war cars were a common sight until the early 1960s. Many garages specialized in repairing the older models. The author worked for a while for the Bugatti and GN expert Stafford East in the late 1950s. He remembers the workshop being filled with an OE 30/98 belonging to well-known Vintage Vauxhall racer Mike Quartermain, a DY saloon in for a decoke and a late 1920s Sunbeam that required new shock absorbers – all in the same week. He also remembers spending a week cleaning an old 1920s Vauxhall crankcase, only to be told it was the wrong one! Here we see L types being crated for export, between September and December 1948.

An export E-type Wyvern at Dinant on the River Meuse in Belgium, 1952. Here the river flows past the massive rock of Dinant which is crowned with an ancient fort. The E type was a popular car in the Low Countries.

An early E-type Velox at The Cross in Malta, 1954. The Cross is the island's war memorial to men and women killed in the Second World War. In the background to the left of the picture is a selection of Malta's wonderful old buses.

With the introduction of the E type a number of the six-cylinder models were entered by private owners for events such as the Monte Carlo Rally and, later in the decade, the Safari Rally in Kenya. The short stroke six-cylinder engine was capable of producing 100 bhp with some tuning. At the time GM did not support motor sport so the trophies went to teams from Ford, Rootes and BMC. These two photographs show a Cresta that was entered in the 1955 Monte Carlo Rally – one taken on the rally and one outside the Vauxhall Works. Notice the modified grille incorporating extra driving lights and also the bug deflector on the leading edge of the bonnet.

A 1956 Velox, entered in the 1958 Monte Carlo Rally. The car was prepared by Shaw & Kilburn Ltd of Wardour Street, London, and their press release read as follows:

It is now common knowledge that the 1958 Monte Carlo Rally was one of the toughest ever, and to reach their destination after traversing ice-covered terrain was no mean achievement. One London entry, which set off from Glasgow, was a 1956 Vauxhall Velox driven by company director Mr E. Brett and his co-driver Dr D. Segall. This car was prepared in the West End service station of our London area dealers, Shaw & Kilburn Ltd, Wardour Street, W1, with very little deviation from standard specification, although special attention was given to engine tuning, brakes and suspension. Also, in order to provide more stability for driver and navigator, the front seat was stiffened and Michelin X tyre equipment was fitted. Apart from a few incidentals the car was in every way standard. Naturally the accepted navigation aids were employed, and Messrs AC Delco kindly provided a specially calibrated speedometer, for use in conjunction with the Halda computer. Ice finding its way into the distributor caused one or two impromptu stops, which resulted in car no. 205 reaching Monte Carlo two hours adrift of its scheduled time. When one remembers the great names in rallying who fell by the wayside, this in itself is no mean achievement. Both Mr Brett and his partner are extremely pleased with the results of their endeavours, especially as this was their first 'Monte', and we at Shaw & Kilburn are more than proud to have been associated with this venture. Plans are already in the air for a PA type to be journeying in 1959 towards Monte Carlo and a coveted award.

A 1957 Velox, showing the new grille and enlarged windscreen.

The underbonnet layout of the 1957 Velox. This engine was also fitted in the Series I PA models.

All crated up for export, 22 October 1956: a 1957 E-type Cresta, showing the colour flash along the side of the car. Before being shipped the framework of the crate would be covered with the large panels seen in the background on the left of the photograph.

The F-type Victor very quickly became Britain's number one export car, as overseas buyers liked the car's styling. The new model had better roadholding, braking and steering than rivals from Rootes, Standard and BMC. Its one failing was the body's tendency to rust. This photo shows an early Super in Switzerland.

Another export Victor Super, this time in Baltimore, Maryland, USA. In the North American market the Victor was sold by Pontiac dealers.

An early example of the Victor estate car on British plates in Spain. The Victor estate car was the first such design from Vauxhall Motors. It was a good looking design, but is now very rare in the UK.

An Irish entry in the 1959 Rallye Monte Carlo, with the then current Victor Super.

The 1959 Victor had smoother styling but lost some of its character. The setting is the Mont Blanc range, seen from the lower bends of the Petit St Bernard pass, above Pre St Didier Courmayeur in the middle distance.

An early example of a PA Cresta. The early cars had a chromium-plated moulding over the gutter, as seen here. The early PA was David Jones's masterpiece, one of the best-looking British cars with its sleek low lines. Nearly forty years later it still looks fresh.

A beautiful car in a wonderful setting: an early PA on the road leading to the Julier Pass in Switzerland. Later cars received a one-piece rear window and the final design lost its purity with larger tail fins, redesigned bumpers and tail lights, plus imitation wood (the type that grows in a metal press) on the facia and door cappings.

# 1961–1970: BREAKING NEW GROUND

It is often wrongly assumed that the FB Victor was less American in its general appearance than the F type. In the late '50s Harley Earl retired and his position was taken by Bill Mitchell, who soon made his name on both sides of the Atlantic. GM's new designs for the 1961 season were neat and generally of very pleasing appearance; the new Vauxhall Victor embodied the new GM concept of car styling. The design was first shown to John Gordon, new president of GM, on his visit to Luton in 1959. Although some engineers at General Motors, including Maurice Olley, were keen on a rear engine layout such as that in the elegant Chevrolet Corvair, introduced to the public in the autumn of 1959, Vauxhall wisely decided to stay with a conventional layout.

The FB range consisted of five models: the Victor estate (FBW), Victor saloon (FBS), Victor de luxe saloon (FBE), Victor de luxe estate (FBG), Victor super saloon (FBD) and the VX4/90 (FBH). This new range, with the exception of the VX4/90, was advertised as 'The clean line of good design and all the qualities of a fine car'.

Mechanically the FB range was very similar to the preceeding F type. The VX4/90 had a tuned engine and was introduced, four weeks after other models in the range, in October 1961, although production did not get under way until January of the following year. The VVX4/90 was the first sporty Vauxhall since the OE 30/98. When launched, the tuned 1505 cc engine produced 70 bhp compared with 50 bhp for other models in the FB range. The VX had a four-speed all-syncromesh gearbox and disc brakes on the front wheels. The tuned engine was fitted with an alloy cylinder head and twin Zenith carburettors. Red gloss paint was applied to the block, sump timing chain cover and rocker cover.

A four-speed all-syncromesh gearbox was optional on the Victor range. Both the de luxe and the VX4/90 had individual front seats. On the Victor de luxe the seats were leather-covered but on the VX4/90 vinyl trim was surprisingly the only option; the rear seat on the VX was moulded to give the appearance of two seats. All models had a neat facia, the VX being fitted with a rev counter, and the facia of the early VX4/90s was finished in wood effect as opposed to the anodised alloy of the Victor models.

Two-tone colour schemes were still popular in the early '60s. On the Victor de luxe, the contrasting colour was applied to the roof, while on the VX4/90 a stylish 'flash' in contrasting colour enlivened the side flanks. The effect in both cases was very pleasant.

The VX4/90 sold very well. By September 1962 the 10,000th example had been produced. If the VX4/90 had one failing it was the gearchange: the mechanism was connected to the gearbox by side levers, and when the linkage became slightly worn changing gear was like stirring a rice pudding. The same comments apply to all post-F type Vauxhalls with four-speed floor gear change!

For the final year of FB production revised specifications were introduced in time for the London Motor Show. The most obvious changes were a new more elaborate grille in anodized aluminium on Victor models and wood trim on the facia of the Victor de luxe. The VX4/90 square rear number plates were fitted to the Series II models, while acrylic paint was used for the first time on the bodywork. The de luxe was also given new front seats, which were extremely comfortable.

The engines were enlarged to 1595 cc for the Victor range and the bhp was increased to 69 at 4800 rpm. The VX4/90 now produced 81 bhp, with a top speed approaching 90 mph, approximately 10 mph faster than the Victor, while the 0–50 times for the respective models were 12.7 seconds and 10.3 seconds.

The Victor estate car was very popular, offering a useful amount of space within a compact body, ideal for carrying larger families and dogs.

At the same time as the FB Victor and VX4/90 range was being designed, Vauxhall's engineering staff were preparing drawings and specifications for the new six-cylinder car designed to take the place of the existing PA range.

With the forthcoming PB and to a slightly lesser extent with the FB, efforts were made to reduce rust. Involved in this programme with David Jones was Gerald Palmer, who had joined Vauxhall Motors in late 1955 from BMC, where he had been technical manager of the BMC Engineering Group. He had originally joined the Nuffield Group from Jowett, where he had almost single-handedly designed the Jowett Javelin. With the PB, efforts were made to avoid crevices and corners which can all too easily trap salt and snow. The sills were to be sprayed with a polythene wax and the lower surfaces of the front and rear wings were to receive a coating of bituminous plastic.

The PB Velox and Cresta were launched at the 1962 Motor Show. Styling was very similar to the FB range; in fact the doors and sills were shared, although the PB was longer and wider than the FB range. The styling was conservative and restrained, but the PB was the nicest looking car in its class. Although in most respects the new range was designed around the mechanical units of the 2.6-litre PA, the PB had power assisted brakes as standard. The interior of both models was well finished, with a facia in burr walnut. The speedometer was of a similar design to that fitted in the 2.6-litre PA, changing from green to orange to red as the road speed increased. Bench seats were standard, those on the Velox being finished in a vinyl known as Ambela. The Cresta had leather trim on the seats, also thicker carpet and underfelt. Externally, the two-tone effect was available on the Cresta; the darker colour on the roof suited the styling very well. As with the previous models, overdrive and Hydramatic automatic transmission were available at extra cost.

The London coachbuilder Harold Radford produced a special luxury version of the Cresta between October 1963 and October 1964. The exterior was given a special paint finish, while the interior featured individual front seats, folding tables at the rear, extra lights, fancy wheel trim, folding sunshine roof, and a silver panel between the rear lights. There was even a chauffeur's division between the front and rear seat. Other features included an all transistor radio and reading lamps. At the end of 1963 a smart estate car joined the PB range. This was finished and trimmed by the old established coachbuilder Martin Walter of Folkestone, better known for the famous Dormobile, which was a conversion based on the Bedford CA van. In appearance the PB estate car followed the lines of the FB estate. The rear roof section and tailgate were made of fibreglass. With 67 cu ft of luggage space, the PB estate car was a useful addition to the range. The 2.6-litre PB had a top speed of around 92 mph and could reach 50 mph in 10 seconds while returning 22 mpg.

For the final season the Vauxhall 2.6-litre engine was replaced by a Chevrolet 3.3-litre unit, which produced 128 bhp against 113 bhp for the previous engine. The top speed increased to 98 mph and the fuel consumption dropped to around 20 mpg. The only styling changes were a bright metal rubbing strip down the side of the car and a rather hideous chromium-plated grille which replaced the previous stylish design. The rear axle ratio on the estate cars was lowered and there was the option of a four-speed gearbox with floor change. There were also two-speed wipers and acrylic paintwork. Another retrograde step was the fitting of the two-speed Powerglide automatic transmission.

Towards the end of the '50s, the company's new manufacturing facilities were in place. It was accepted by General Motors in Detroit and the management at Luton that any increase in the company's models would be in the small car market. Opel in Germany was thinking along the same lines. At this time Vauxhall and Opel were expected to compete in export markets – and Vauxhall's chief engineer, Maurice Platt, regarded his opposite number at Opel, Karl Stief, as a friendly rival. Discussion took place between Philip Copenlin, Maurice Platt, David Jones and Gerald Palmer. The conclusion was reached that a considerable amount of time and money would be saved if the new small car were developed with Opel. A representation was made to John Gordon and Pete Hoglund on 1 October 1960 and the project was given the go-ahead. The next stage was the construction of a styling model in fibreglass by David Jones and his department, for presentation before the president and members of the Overseas Policy Group on 8 March in the following year.

A change in Vauxhall's MD came about when Phillip Copenlin was replaced by William Swallow on 1 April 1961. Swallow, a Yorkshireman, had been Managing Director of GM since 1956.

In the late '50s and early '60s Vauxhall had been testing various types of independent rear suspension. Some company engineers had thought that the new small car could feature this idea, but in the event it was decided to stay with a solid axle and leaf springs. In preparing the Vauxhall version of the new car, Opel's drawings were studies. There was no attempt to achieve interchangeability of components made in both Britain and Germany; all metric dimensions and standards were converted into inches, including screw threads. In the following decade metric measurements became standard for all GM cars and trucks.

At the time that development of the new small car was proceeding, work had also begun (in 1961) on a £66 million investment at Ellesmere Port. The 393-acre site on Merseyside would eventually become home for the new design, the Viva, employing some 10,000 staff by the end of the 1960s; this compared with approximately 18,500 at Luton and 5,700 at Bedford and the replacement parts operation at Dunstable in the same period.

By the early 1960s Opel was using larger than usual sheet steel pressings to construct the integral bodies of its cars. The result was fewer welds and greater accuracy in body construction, ensuring a good fit for doors and glass.

William Swallow chose the name Viva for the new car, which went into production in September 1963. In some export territories, such as France, Canada and Australia, the car was known as the Epic. This small car, also assembled in Antwerp, Copenhagen, Berne, Melbourne, Port Elizabeth and Wellington, had a square plain appearance. Its dimensions were almost identical to the Vauxhall 10 of twenty-six years earlier, although 10 in lower. Known as the HA type, the first Viva was available in basic and de luxe specifications. It proved to be very popular, with 100,000 being built in the first ten months of production and 303,738 by the time production ceased in March 1966.

The new small Vauxhall used the Opel Kadett floor pan, suspension, brakes, engine, gearbox and rear axle. It was advertised as having 'the millionaire ride', and had a 29 ft turning circle, 10½ cubic ft of luggage space, a top speed of 80 mph and room for four big people. Most people will remember the HA for its very light steering combined with 40 mpg. The ride was unremarkable and the handling not the car's strong point. For an extra £12 you could specify front disc brakes. At £527 7s 11d, including purchase tax, or £566 1s 3d for the de luxe, which had a heater and windscreen washers, the Viva was faster through the gears and had more room for luggage than the opposition, as well as being reliable – something not necessarily found elsewhere.

The engine was an Opel design and had pressed steel rockers for the first time on a European GM unit. The standard compression was 8.5:1, although 7.3:1 was available for areas where only low octane fuel could be bought. The three-bearing 1057 cc engine proved 44 bhp at 5200 rpm, both at the standard compression ratio. The front suspension was unusual in that it used double wishbones combined with a traverse leaf spring. The gearbox was a four-speed all-syncromesh unit with a very pleasant remote control gear lever.

Further editions arrived in 1965 with the SL followed in the autumn by the 90 models; the de luxe 90 and the SL 90. The SL (super luxury) was fitted with good quality carpet, extra padding on the facia and a fussier grille, with twin aluminium side mouldings down the side of the vehicle. The 90 received a red painted engine producing 60 bhp. On these faster Vivas the disc brakes were standard, as was a reinforced propshaft. Early examples of the 90 suffered from problems with the inlet manifold hot spot. This was accompanied by chronic misfiring, which was resolved by replacing the inlet manifold. Generally, however, the HA models were reliable.

Introduced in time for the 1964 Motor Show was the new FC type, replacing the FB. The new Victor range was known as the 101. The designation was only a figure, and had no connection with the vehicle design. In the salesman's handbook for the 101 range it referred to the number as a way of easy recognition, suggesting that following models could be 102, 103 and so on. In the event this did not happen.

The new design was totally different from its predecessor, with curved side windows, a concave rear window and flush sides, which in profile showed a gentle curve. It was a stylish car, but its appearance was spoilt by the design of the anodized aluminium grille on the Series I and VX4/90. In all, six models were offered: the standard saloon, super saloon, de luxe saloon, estate car, estate car de luxe and VX4/90. Prices ranged from £678 4s 7d for the standard saloon to £871 11s 3d for the VX4/90.

Compared with the opposition the Victor 101 offered more space, a better ride and modern appearance. The main mechanical units wre taken from the previous FB range. Self-adjusting drum brakes were used all round, with power-assisted discs on the front as an optional feature but fitted as standard on the VX4/90. The body was protected with underbody seal at the factory and acrylic paint was standard.

Internally de luxe models and VX4/90s had heater ducts to the rear. Standard saloons had bench seats covered in vinyl, whereas the de luxe version and the VX4/90 had separate front seats, also covered with vinyl. Leather seat trim was optional on the de luxe models. The de luxe and VX4/90 featured cutpile carpets. In the case of the VX4/90 a revised facia was used, with gauges for water temperature, ampères and oil pressure, in addition to a rev counter and speedometer. On the de luxe models a piece of polished wood replaced the anodized aluminium moulding. In autumn 1966 a much improved restyled grille appeared on the standard, super and de luxe models, with small variations to trim and changes to seat design. At the same time the compression ratio was increased from 8.5:1 to 9:1, resulting in a rise in bhp from 70 to 76. On the VX4/90 the bhp was now 81 – and the later 101 VX4/90s were even fitted with limited slip differential. The VX4/90 had a four-speed all-syncromesh gearbox with floor change, while the other models in the 101 range had a choice of the four-speed unit, a three-speed with column change or the two-speed Powerglide automatic transmission. The VX4/90 was flat out at 90 mph, whilst the other models were about 10 mph slower. 0–60 was achieved in 18 seconds and 21 seconds respectively.

The 101 range was very popular in its day with 219,814 101 Victors and 13,449 101 VX4/90s produced. It was a good reliable car, cornering well apart from the initial roll – although it is possible to lose the back end of the 101 VX4/90 on twisty wet roads.

For Vauxhall, the period between 1958 and 1967 had been the most financially successful in the firm's history. In 1964 Vauxhall Motors made a profit of £17.9 million.

On 31 August 1963 Maurice Platt retired. He was now sixty-five years of age and under company rules it was mandatory. He was replaced by John Alden, who had originally joined the company in 1938 after serving an apprenticeship with MG at Abingdon. During the Second World War he was in charge of experimental testing and development of Bedford army trucks. In 1956 he was promoted to the position of Commercial Vehicle Engineer, and by 1963 he had been given the new title of Chief Product Engineer, having overall responsibility for the design and development of cars, trucks, bus and coach chassis. In his late thirties Alden developed the famous Bedford TK, which for many years was Britain's most popular truck, in both home and export markets. He was highly competent, a man of drive and stamina.

In October 1965 the first of the new PC six-cylinder cars were launched. As with the last PB types, the PC models were powered by a Chevrolet engine. The name Velox was dropped on the new range, and the first two models were the Cresta (replacing the Velox) and the Cresta de luxe. In 1966 the Viscount was introduced as the most luxurious Vauxhall of the period. The engine had been first used in the 1965 PB Velox and Cresta. It was of typical GM design with pushrod-operated ohv and four-bearing crankshaft. It was durable and robust but at high revs the lack of a seven-bearing bottom was evident. Not for the first time, David Jones and his team produced the most attractive design in its class, the elegant restrained lines clearly influenced by Bill Mitchell's designs in the States. The door pressings were shared with the Victor 101 range. The car's width was reduced by 1 in and the length increased by 5 in. Taking advantage of the curved door profile, there was no loss of interior width; there were also more substantial bumpers and a neat grille of horizontal bars in addition to dual headlights on the Cresta de luxe, while the Cresta was fitted with single headlights. The Viscount had a grille of extruded aluminium featuring horizontal and vertical bars in addition to a handsome vinyl roof. Three types of wheel trim were fitted to the PC range. The Cresta was fitted with chrome hub caps, on the Cresta de luxe there were also anodized wheel trims, and on the Viscount chrome hub caps and wheel rings. The Cresta de luxe came with white wall tyres, although during the '60s the width of white rubber was much reduced. The Viscount was supplied with black wall tyres, as was the Cresta.

The interior trim was of good quality. Wood trim was applied to the lower half of the facia on the Cresta and Cresta de luxe, while the Viscount received additional wood trim to the upper half of the facia and the door panels. On the Cresta a vinyl (Ambela) covered bench seat was standard while on the de luxe individual front seats were fitted, with the option of leather seat trim. Heavier carpet was used on the De Luxe and the Viscount, which had leather seat trim and reclining front seats with Chapman Reuter mechanism. The extra sound deadening and equipment on the Viscount increased its overall weight by

220 lb, cutting the top speed from 103 mph to 97 mph. Power steering was standard on the Viscount, together with automatic transmission and powered windows; a few Viscounts were supplied with the floor-mounted four-speed gearbox at a saving of £85. This gearbox was an option on the other two models in place of the standard three-speed column-mounted gear change. Until 1970 the Viscount used the Powerglide two-speed automatic transmission. Disc front brakes were fitted on all models. The Cresta would reach 60 mph in 12½ seconds. All models would return between 19 and 23 mpg, the Powerglide automatic versions being the most uneconomical. The brakes were good and the handling safe, although 5.90–14 tyres seem rather small section by today's standards.

In 1967 Martin Walker produced a factory approved estate car conversion of the Cresta de luxe. As with the previous design for the PB range, the rear roof section was made of fibreglass. Some of these estate cars were supplied to the police for motorway work. For the last two years of production the Powerglide was replaced by the vastly superior three-speed GM 'Strasbourg' automatic transmission.

Production of these last British-built and designed large Vauxhalls ceased in 1972. In service the cars were generally reliable, but towards the end of the '60s British component manufacturers had a spotty reliability record which could be reflected in small annoying problems. There was one failing which anyone who worked in a Vauxhall service department will remember: the exhaust system would sag in the middle where the single down pipe branched into two tail pipes.

In all, 53,912 Crestas were produced and 7,025 Viscounts. When launched, a Cresta de luxe cost £1058 17s 1d and a Viscount £1,457 12s 1d.

The HB Viva introduced in March 1966 took the best features from the previous HA type and added first class all coil suspension, much improved rack and pinion steering, vastly improved trim and most noticeable of all, a really elegant body that put all the opposition in the shade! In all, there were twenty-six variations of the HB Viva. The model was Vauxhall's sales success of the '60s, with half a million sold worldwide in only four years. David Jones' styling took the proportions of the PC and scaled them down very successfully. Three engine sizes covered the range; 1159 cc, ohc 1599 cc and ohc 1975 cc. The 47 bhp 1159 cc unit and the 83 bhp 1599 cc were available with Borg Warner automatic transmission (three-speed). The tuned versions of these engines were not supplied from the factory with automatic transmission.

The new Viva was 6½ in longer than its predecessor and the weight had increased from 1564 lb to 1704 lb (two-door standard). In designing it John Alden's aim was to improve standards of refinement, safety and reliability. For the majority of drivers the most noticeable improvement, apart from styling, was in road holding and handling. The roll axis had been revised (this is the axis about which the body rolls): the longitudinal axis was raised by 4.75 in; thus the distance between the spring centre of gravity and the roll axis was reduced. The result was a roll moment (the force that makes a car roll) 25 per cent lower than on the HA Viva. On the road a driver would experience 33 per cent less roll at normal speeds and approximately 10 per cent less at high speeds. In short, the HB was fun to drive on a twisty route, whereas the HA was not. The ohv-engined models also had an improved water pump which incorporated the thermostat and fan and was mounted on the cylinder head, thereby eliminating the need for a backplate. In addition the fan size was reduced to lessen vibration and for most markets a two-blade fan replaced the earlier four-blade unit. The use of a two-blade fan resulted partly from an improved radiator which was of tube and centre contruction. This offered less restriction to the coolant and air flow. The coolant was pressurised at 13 psi instead of 7, thus raising the boiling point. The optional disc brakes were fitted with larger calipers and the friction pad area was increased. On the gearbox the rear cover and mainshaft were increased in length, while the propshaft was shortened and received improved dynamic balancing. The end result was longer life for drive train components.

At the beginning of 1967 a Borg Warner automatic was offered as an optional extra. At the same time a Jack Brabham engine conversion was available through Vauxhall dealers. The 1159 cc Viva 90 was tuned to produce 79 bhp (thanks to a modified cylinder head); it also carried twin carburettors, new manifold and straight through silencer, plus body strips.

In June 1967 the three-door estate car was introduced. Loads of up to 5 ft in length could be accommodated. March 1968 saw the introduction of the 112 bhp Viva GT, powered by an 1975 cc ohc slant four-cylinder engine with five-bearing crankshaft and hemispherical head. The top speed was 104 mph with 0–60 achieved in 11.4 seconds. The MK I GT was rather conspicuous with its matt black bonnet. With extra tuning from Bill Blydenstein, the model was also capable of further performance.

The '60s had seen the return of Vauxhall to the racing circuit, although many 30/98s have been, and still are, entered in events regularly by their enthusiastic owners. Gerry Marshall took the Griffin to glory many times during the '60s and '70s with cars ranging from tuned VX4/90s and ohc Vivas to the famous Big Bertha, powered by a 5-litre 445 bhp Repco Holden V8.

In June 1968 the Viva range expanded still further with two additional four-door saloons and a three-door estate car powered by the 1599 cc 83 bhp ohc engine. Two levels of trim were offered, De Luxe and SL. These models were joined by four-door versions of the 1159 cc-powered models, the De Luxe, 90 De Luxe SL and the SL 90. The final addition to the HB range was the Mark II Viva GT, which had a toned down exterior and Rostyle wheels.

The Brabham conversion on the Viva 90 and SL 90 ceased after 1968. The last of the smart Crayford convertibles was produced in September 1970. Production of all other variations of the HB Viva stopped in the same month to make way for the new HC Viva. The HB range had been a big success for Vauxhall Motors at a time when the sales of larger models had sometimes dropped behind those of competitors.

The problems with the inlet manifold persisted for a while on the ohv engine models. The ohc models were rather noisy inside, the gearchange on manual gearbox versions was never very good and the GT suffered from clutch problems. The ohc engines also suffered with oil leaks and it was not unknown for the timing belt to slip a few teeth! Even so, a well-tuned Viva GT has much to commend it.

1967 was Vauxhall Motors' Diamond Jubilee year. In October of that year the company launched the new FD Victor range at the London Motor Show. The range consisted of two engine sizes, 1559 cc and 1975 cc. The stylish body was noted for its thin windscreen pillars. Lower by 1.4 in and longer by almost 2 in than the old model, the new design was praised by the national press. 'The star of the show', said *The Times*; 'British car of the year', said the *Sunday Times*. In addition, the Victor 2000 was awarded the Don Safety Trophy for contributing most to road safety during the year.

The FD was fitted with the new ohc slant four, also used in the larger engine Vivas. On paper the new engine was a winner but, as mentioned earlier, not without problems. The previous ohv engine used in the 101 range had been a simple but effective design. From the driver's point of view it was a very flexible unit which was easy to service and long lasting.

The 1600 followed previous base model Victors in having a front bench seat, drum brakes with option of disc front brakes and a three-speed gearbox with column gear change. All the FD range were fitted with rack and pinion steering and all coil spring suspension. As with the new HB Viva, the rear axle was well positioned. Both the roadholding and steering were excellent. A four-headlamp system was used for the first time. The Victor 2000 SL had disc front brakes, individual front seats, four-speed gearbox with floor change and the optional fitting of an overdrive unit which was controlled by a switch on the gear lever knob. Unfortunately, all too often the knob worked loose, the wire to the switch became entangled and the driver found himself with overdrive in reverse! As a result of the new suspension design, the ride was harder. The newly designed front seats were also firmer than those fitted to the FB Victor de luxe or the FC Victor de luxe. As a result, the inviting looking seats proved to be not to everyone's taste. Incidentally, the front bench seat on the 1600 was worse!

The Victor FD was one of those cars which with a few modifications could have been much more successful than it was. It needed better seats, a proper remote control four-speed gear change, a good three-speed automatic transmission (which came in January 1970) and a revised linkage for the three-speed column gearbox. An engine developed by Bill Blydenstein would also have shown the vehicle's potential.

The other FD models were the estate car versions, the six-cylinder Ventora and the VX4/90. The estate car, introduced in May 1968, like the saloon was stylish. It could accommodate 60.5 cubic ft of luggage. Like its saloon counterparts it featured a collapsible steering column, plus the faulty design features mentioned earlier. It was possible to specify the 3.3-litre six-cylinder Chevrolet engine which was very reliable. However, early six-cylinder examples suffered with a low overall gearing, as did the Series I Ventora. In automatic form, the Powerglide was the only option until the advent of the excellent three-speed Strasbourg-built GM automatic from January 1970. The VX4/90 version of the FD range was introduced at the Paris Motor Show in October 1969, although deliveries did not start until February of the following year. When production ceased twenty-four months later, some 14,277 VX4/90s had been produced, 828 more than the FC VX4/90. The twin carburettor 2-litre engine was the same as used in the Viva GT. It gave the new sporting Vauxhall a top speed of 97 mph, combined with an average fuel consumption of 21 mpg. The facia had a full array of instruments and the floor was covered in deep pile carpet. Fuel consumption could be improved by specifying the optional overdrive. As with the Series II Viva GT, Rostyle wheels were fitted as standard equipment.

Following the FD Victor by six months was the Ventora, which used the 3294 cc Chevrolet engine. The Ventora was without doubt the best of the FD range. The Series I suffered from low gearing, and like the rest of the FD and PC ranges at the time the automatic option was Powerglide, which meant that the engine sounded rather fussy above 60 mph. The interior featured an attractive facia with a full range of instruments including a rev counter. Quality carpet lined the floor and as for other FDs the door trims were one-piece plastic mouldings. The only extra needed, apart from overdrive, was a radio. Like other FD models you sat on rather than in the seats! Externally the Ventora was identified by a smart vinyl roof which suited the car very well, cheese cutter grille and handsome stainless steel wheel trims. The Ventora was well received. For £1,101 the car offered good performance (0–60 in just over 11 seconds) and 20 plus mpg at a top speed of around 103 mph, combined with excellent handling, steering and braking.

In October 1969 the Series II Ventora was introduced. The overall gearing was increased, pushing the top speed up to 106 mph. The front seats now reclined, the rear bench seat was redesigned to resemble two individual seats, along the lines of the Rover 2000. Reversing lights were now standard, as was a heated rear window. The greatest improvement was the replacing of the Powerglide automatic transmission by the three-speed Strasbourg-built GM automatic. A Series II automatic Ventora is one of the most under-rated cars of the late 1960s.

The Series II PA was still a sleek good-looking car. At the Torino Automobile Show in November 1959 there was a parade of all GM 1960 models during the GM press reception.

The following year another parade of GM cars took place, this time of 1961 models. Shown here are the final designs for the PA and F types.

The FB Victor was a good-looking car. This is the Super of 1961. The new design was roomier and had a larger boot than the F type. The basic model had no bright mouldings around the front and rear windows. All FBs and FCs had a pleasant and distinctive exhaust note, owing to the use of a silencer that, it was claimed, offered less back pressure to the exhaust gases.

A Series I FB VX4/90 outside Stockholm Town Hall, August 1962. Cars for the British market were not fitted with white wall tyres. The VX4/90 was the first Vauxhall to win races since the 30/98. The car was developed by Bill Blydenstein and Chris Lawrence from 1962 onwards. 1963 saw the VX4/90 in third place in the European Challenge Cup. After this success Blydenstein branched out on his own. He was later joined by Don Hagger. By the end of 1971 Bill Blydenstein and his small team had shown that the Vauxhall could again be a very successful car in the competition field. Taking 1971 as an example, the Blydenstein stable, together with Dealer Team Vauxhall, which was formed in July 1971, had eighteen outright wins, thirteen class wins and established six outright records, plus seven class records in hill climbs. Had Bill Blydenstein been put in charge of engine and chassis development at Luton, Vauxhall might have become the centre of GM European design. There were other tuners who offered modified parts for the VX4/90; these included Mangoletsi who extracted 96 bhp from the 1508 cc unit on the dynamometer when preparing cars for the *Motor* Six Hour Production Car race. Another well-known VX4/90 specialist at this time was Lawrence Tune Engines Ltd of Acton.

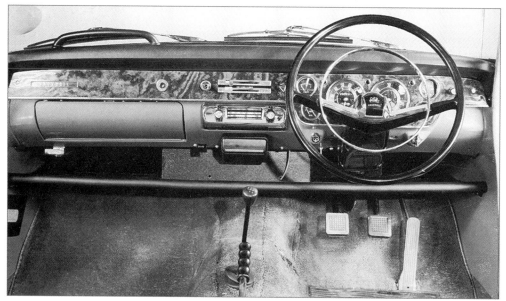

The neat design of the 1964 VX4/90's facia is well illustrated in this photograph. The repositioned panel control knobs were now within easy reach of a driver wearing a safety belt. The 1964 models had simplified heater controls and a grab handle for the passenger. All 1964 FB models were finished in acrylic paint. The finish at first was not as good as on preceding models.

The offside of the engine bay showing the brake servo heater hoses, battery and the offside of the engine. Notice the felt applied to the bulkhead, designed to act as a sound deadener.

The 1964 Victor de luxe can be identified by its fussier anodized aluminium grille and painted centres of the hub caps with the Vauxhall griffin badge. The two-tone paint suited the car very well. Leather-covered seats were standard, as was polished wood trim on the facia. The front seats were very comfortable. Again Vauxhall had produced the best in its class. This left-hand drive car is parked beside the Dead Sea at 1,286 ft below sea level. The clifftop fortress of Massada is on the right.

The new HA Viva had light controls and more space for passengers and luggage than its competitors. For many years the van version of the HA was very popular with Royal Mail. This is the Viva de luxe, identified by the bright moulding along the sides. This example was photographed in January 1966 at Liverpool and destined for Canada.

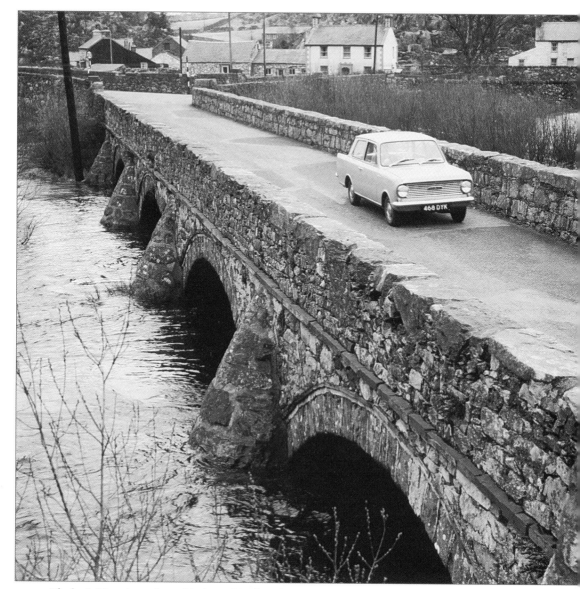

The basic Viva pictured near Llanberis, North Wales.

An export PB-type Velox, 1964 model, photographed in May of the previous year at Luton. Notice the wing mirror – only one on the offside. The author restored a right-hand drive example of the PB Velox in the early 1980s for everyday use. When taken to shows the car caused a surprising amount of interest: when did you last see a tidy PB Velox or Cresta?

The Martin Walter estate car conversion on the PB-type Cresta resulted in a smart looking vehicle. Series I PB Cresta saloons did not have the bright strip down the flanks of the car. The Series II with revised grille did adopt this moulding.

The Vauxhall Radford: two photographs of this rare conversion of the PB Cresta by Harold Radford
Coachbuilders Ltd.

A FC Victor 101 Super, March 1965. The FC was 1½ in longer than the FB and just over ½ in wider. Owing to the curved body sides there was a gain of 4 in in shoulder room. Although the platform remained much as before, the new body was a lot more rigid; in fact, some 28 per cent in bending and 70 per cent in torsion. The new body was 60 lb heavier.

A prototype export VX4/90 (FC), June 1964. Production models had a flash down the flanks of the body in a contrasting colour. As with other FC models, the whole underbody was sprayed with a ⅛ in coat of heavy bituminous sealer. This was applied to both sides of the steel floor. The box beams under the door sills were sprayed internally with a bituminous aluminium compound.

Some export territories had regulations which required vehicles to be a maximum length. This Victor 101 estate with its foreshortened nose was photographed in Bermuda. The new Victor 101 estate car was 4 in longer than before and the rear tailgate had a redesigned torsion bar counterbalance spring which decreased the stress. The forward-hinged quarterlights were designed to eliminate wind noise.

The PC range shared all the advantages of the FC: stiffer body shell and better looks. The PC Cresta's and Viscount's direct competitors were the ungainly Mk IV Ford Zephyr and Zodiac ranges which were launched on 20 April 1966. David Jones's styling deserves greater recognition. Thirty years later the PC still looks elegant.

The Martin Walter estate car conversion was well done. Today these cars are quite rare; production of the estate car finished in 1968 after only three years. Its replacement was the FD-type Victor 3300 estate car.

The Viscount was the last of the traditional big Vauxhalls designed and built in Britain. Early cars suffered from Powerglide automatic transmission; however, a four-speed manual gearbox was available at no extra cost. Later cars were fitted with the excellent GM three-speed Strasbourg automatic transmission.

The interior of the Viscount was very inviting, with burr walnut on the facia and door panels, leather-covered seats and quality carpet. The comprehensive specification included power steering and windows, reclining seats, radio, heated rear window and map reading light. Today, the Viscount makes a very sensible classic car; it has all the luxury of a Jaguar and is much easier to work on.

Vivas for Canada! The HB Viva range of ten models was the best-selling Vauxhall up to that time.

The four-door and two-door SL Vivas were the best appointed and best looking cars in their class. The two-door SL cost £698 13*s* 2*d*, including purchase tax, in October 1967. The HB offered excellent steering and road holding.

The flowing lines of the Viva SL estate car contrast with those of the Liverpool–Dublin ferry.

The Viva GT offered 104 bhp and a top speed of 100 mph. Anyone who worked in a Vauxhall garage at the time will remember that the standard clutch never lasted very long. When the car was tuned by Bill Blydenstein its full potential could be realized.

The FD-type Victor followed the suspension layout of the HB-type Viva. There was rack and pinion steering for the first time on a medium-sized Vauxhall but the four-cylinder never seemed to develop the power claimed, unless you were lucky enough to drive a Blydenstein-modified example. This is a UK specification Victor 2000.

Sweden was a good market for Vauxhall cars. For the period January to September 1968, shipments to Sweden were 50 per cent up on the corresponding period of 1967. The car is a Victor 2000, 1969 model, to Swedish specification. Notice the plain hub caps: British specification 2000s had handsome stainless steel wheel trims. The car is parked at the yacht harbour at Sigtuna, about 30 miles north of Stockholm.

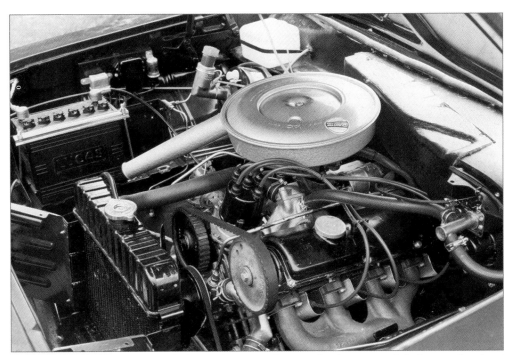

On paper the Victor 2000 engine had everything in its favour – five-bearing crankshaft, cross-flow hemi head, overhead camshaft. Even the exhaust manifold was designed to promote good gas flow. In standard form it lacked the flexibility of the previous design; also oil leaks were a constant problem. It took Bill Blydenstein to release its potential.

The vinyl-covered bench seats fitted to the Victor 1600 were neither very inviting nor very comfortable.

The Vauxhall range on the General Motors stand at the Amsterdam Motor Show, 1 May 1969.

The Ventora had the advantage of the excellent 3.3-litre Chevrolet engine. Series I models were rather low geared. The Series II from 1970 had higher overall gearing and the option of the GM Strasbourg three-speed automatic transmission. Up to 1969 the Vynide roof covering was an option, but from 1969 onwards it became standard. The colour was either black or parchment according to the body colour. These views show how modern the styling of these cars was compared with the opposition.

The Victor 3300 estate replaced the Cresta estate; because of its engine, it was a better buy than the four-cylinder models.

A correctly maintained ohv Vauxhall from the late 1940s and through to the mid-1960s was quite capable of giving over 100,000 miles of service without having to replace the engine or gearbox. Although today many cars are capable of such performance, thirty or forty years ago many makes required a replacement gearbox or engine at 50,000 miles. The author, who served a BMC apprenticeship, remembers customers accepting such poor performance as normal. Here we see Axel Holberg taking delivery of his new Victor 101 Super in 1966. His 1950 L-type Velox had covered 106,000 miles and cost him only £70 in repairs, apart from expendable items such as tyres, exhausts and so on.

# 1971–1978 : MODERN TIMES

FD production ceased in March 1972. A total of 198,085 cars and estate cars were produced. The 1960s was a period of mixed fortunes for both the British motor industry and Vauxhall Motors. In 1960 Britain produced 1,352,728 cars, which was then a record. By the following year the figures had dropped to 1,003,967. For twenty years, thanks to Bartlett's Management Advisory Committee, there were no strikes at Vauxhall Motors. The period between 1965 and 1969 saw a number of industrial disputes; however, the company received the Queen's Award to Industry, and in February 1967 Vauxhall was granted the Royal Warrant as motor vehicle manufacturers to the Queen. In July 1969 Chairman David Hegland announced that one in every six cars sold in Britain was a Vauxhall. Vauxhall Motors' sales success with the Viva range and its Bedford trucks and coach chassis made up for the relatively modest number of larger Vauxhalls sold. In 1967 the company sold 34,722 FD models and 7,287 Cresta and Viscount models.

Between 1969 and 1975 Vauxhall lost £40.6 million. In 1970 only 3,597 Ventoras were registered in the UK. In September 1970 David Hegland stood down and was replaced by Alexander Rhea who, like Hegland, came to Luton from Holden.

In October 1970 the final Viva appeared, the HC. This car would remain in production for nine years and in that time it was offered with a greater choice of body and trim variations than any previous Vauxhall. The new design was 2 in wider and 1 in longer than the HB. It was a neat little car with greater glass area than the HB, thereby creating the impression of greater size. The new car was launched at the Motor Show in Paris. It was a success, like its predecessor. In all, some 640,863 examples were built between October 1970 and June 1979. Four engine sizes were offered, 1159 cc, which was replaced in August 1971 by a large ohv 1256 cc unit. This engine was produced for thirteen years, finally ending production with the very successful Chevette in September 1982. The HC Viva range consisted of two and four-door saloons, a three-door estate car and a two-door coupé.

Larger engine models were initially fitted with a 1599 cc version of the ohc slant four engine, which was replaced in 1972 by a 1759 cc unit producing 88 bhp, 8 more than the smaller engine. Also available was Vauxhall's 110 bhp 2279 cc engine.

There was no direct replacement for the Viva GT, although the Firenza coupé, which was originally powered by the 1159 cc unit and then the 1256 cc unit, followed other models in the HC Viva range by being available with the ohc engine.

Although their production span of only two years (May 1971 to September 1973) was short, the sportier variants have a following over 20 years after. The best known example of the Firenza is probably the HP (High Performance), which would reach 60 in 9.4 seconds and was clocked by *Motor* in 1973 at over 130 mph. The HP used a five-speed gearbox and a streamlined fibreglass nose section known as a droop snoot! Other models in the Firenza range were fitted with a four-speed gearbox or there was the option of a three-speed automatic.

The different engine sizes received different instrument layouts; the sportier versions have full instrumentation. The Dealer Team Vauxhall racing team, formed in 1971, was very successful with a modified Firenza coupé, which had a 2.3-litre engine fitted with a 16-valve cylinder head, driven by Gerry Marshall.

The Viva 2300 and 1800 were developed into the Magnum 2300 and 1800 from 1974 to 1977. The Magnum, although basically a Viva, was the last completely British design from Vauxhall.

Because of poor sales of the HP Firenza and the coupé version of the Magnum, the company used the existing bodyshell to produce an economy model, the Viva E, powered by the OHV 1256 cc engine. Later an E version of the two- and four-door saloon was produced.

The final Victor/Ventora VX4/90 was the FE type introduced in March 1972. Production of the FE VX4/90 finished in the summer of 1978, while the Victor and Ventora remained in production until January 1976. With the introduction of the FE, Vauxhall returned to the traditional grille and flutes. The author's friend, the late Geoffrey King, always said that this was because the FE was David Jones' last design before retiring; nostalgia for the past. The styling of the FE was simple and elegant with a large window area. The Vauxhall grille and flutes made a welcome change from the bland shapes now appearing from most, if not all, medium price manufacturers. Mechanically, the FE followed the pattern of the FD range, except that the floor plan was shared with the Opel Rekord. The new models were not only roomier than their predecessors, but were more spacious than any direct rival from Ford, Chrysler UK or British Leyland. The estate car had a sloping tailgate which, while stylish, reduced the loading capacity. Although the all coil suspension gave good roadholding, the 1800 and 2300 slant four engines were still not as lively as rival engines from Ford or Chrysler UK.

The Victor range was available in the basic 1800 version, which had a bench front seat when first introduced. In September 1972 this was replaced by separate seats. the 2300 SL was powered by the 110 bhp 2279 cc engine, which although sluggish in standard form did have excellent pulling power. At the 1974 London Motor Show the 2300 S version of the Victor was shown for the first time, featuring a black vinyl roof with (usually) pale blue metallic paintwork, twin coach lines, bright mouldings around wheel arches and a colour matching interior with brushed nylon seat trim. The exterior and interior embellishments suited the car well; the 2300 S was a popular 'special' at the time.

At the launch of the 2300 S, the Vauxhall stand was also used to launch one of the most exciting Vauxhalls of modern times, 'Big Bertha'. This car was designed for racing and was based on the shape of the FD Ventora and powered by a 445 bhp Repco-Holden V8. The car featured a De Dion rear end to reduce unsprung weight. Sadly, the car's racing career was all too short. Driven by Gerry Marshall, it crashed at Silverstone after only six months, when a brake pad fell out. After the crash, the 445 bhp engine was fitted to a Firenza, which was raced with success by Gerry Marshall and known as 'Baby Bertha'.

The new VX4/90 was an improvement on the previous model. The 2279 cc initially produced 110 bhp; two less than the FD's 1975 cc unit but with improved torque. The final Series I FE type VX4/90 1974/5 had its power boosted to 116 bhp. These FE models would reach 60 mph in 11 seconds but the average fuel consumption could be as low as 17 mpg in urban conditions. As with other models in the range, dual circuit brakes made a welcome return. In all, 18,043 VX4/90s were produced between 1972 and 1976. At its launch the price was £1,524 compared with £1,299 for the 2300 SL. There were a number of tuning improvements which were approved by Dealer Team Vauxhall and available from Vauxhall dealers, which improved the performance of the VX4/90. The model won the 1974 Repco Caravan Racing Championship.

The four-cylinder FE range was modified for its final two years of production. By January 1976 the models were known as the VX 1800 and VX 2300. Externally there were larger headlamps and a less attractive grille. The VX 1800 received anodized aluminium trim around the window frames for the first time. On the VX 2300 an anti-roll bar was fitted. The saloons were finished in ribbed velour upholstery. Until March 1977 the estate cars used Ambla, when velour was then used across the range.

The Ventora was by far the best of the FE range with its trusty 3.3-litre Chevrolet engine. Power rack and pinion steering was standard, as were dual circuit brakes. Later examples had the centre of the grille finished in matt black, as opposed to the silver of the earlier car. Like the 2300s there was a special limited edition of the Ventora, the VIP of 1973, which was only available in black. As with the previous FD Ventora, the FE was fitted with a vinyl roof which suited the styling. A full length rubbing strip protected doors and wings from dents and scratches occurring in car parks, and the wheels were fitted with distinctive hub caps and wheel rings. The facia had a rosewood finish. Like the earlier series there was a six-cylinder estate car, at first badged as the 3300 SL but from October 1973 known as the

Ventora Estate. In January 1976, production of the Ventora ceased and the model was replaced by the distinctive 2300 GLS. With its exclusive extruded aluminium grille, beige coloured vinyl roof and 'extra dark wine' paint, it was a good looking car. The 2300 GLS was provided with a front body spoiler, sill capping, wheel arch capping, halogen headlights and rear door operated courtesy lights. When fitted with the optional GM automatic transmission it was a nice car to drive, the nicest of the four-cylinder VX range.

The Series II VX4/90 was given revised seating, a front air dam and a revised grille, headlights and German Getrag five-speed gearbox also used on the HP Firenza. The Getrag gearbox was a big improvement on the four-speed Vauxhall gearbox used in all manual change FDs. Unlike the Vauxhall gearbox, which still used side linkage, the Getrag had a positive gearchange owing to direct selection. There were changes to the steering wheel and the gauges. After only eleven months production ceased on the final design of the VX4/90. Between 1972 and 1976, 18,042 Series FE VX4/90s had been produced. Of the Series II only around 900 were manufactured between 1977 and 1978.

The FE range was not a sales success. In road reports there were complaints of the noisy gearbox (four-speed), poor gear change and clutch pedals at different heights from the other pedals. The ohc engine had potential but was rather thirsty and the 3.3-litre engine was heavy and outdated with its four-bearing bottom end, although reliable. If only the Ventora and VX4/90 could have had the ex-Buick V8 that GM sold to Rover, coupled to a good five-speed gearbox or four-speed automatic transmission, then the FE story might have had a happier end. The lessons of Alex Taub had been forgotten!

The Viva was replaced by the Chevette, which was the last car badged as a Vauxhall to actually use a Vauxhall engine. Introduced in March 1975, the Chevette was GM's 'T' car, available in different countries under various GM brand names. The car had appeared first in 1974 in Brazil, where a Chevrolet version was sold. In the USA Chevrolet and Pontiac were the brand names; Japan used the Isuzu name; in West Germany it was the Opel; and in Argentina and Britain it was the Chevrolet and Vauxhall respectively. Different markets received different engines, transmissions and styling details.

The success of the Opel-designed Chevette saw the start of Vauxhall's return to profitability and sales success. The range was available as a three-door hatchback (which was in fact the first British-built design of its type), two-door saloon, four-door saloon and estate car with a top speed of around 90 mph. In normal driving conditions 40 mpg was obtainable. The success of the car is shown in the number produced between March 1975 and March 1984, which was 415,608. The range was priced from £1,649 at its launch. The effect of monetary inflation at the time is reflected in the dramatic rise in car prices during this period. In 1972 it was possible to buy a VX4/90 for £1,542! Bright colours, two levels of trim and a fifteen minute promotional film shown at Vauxhall dealers featuring Rodney Bewes from the TV series, *The Likely Lads*, plus some excellent TV advertising, got sales under way. The car had been tested for over one million miles all over the world, including Vauxhall's proving ground at Millbrook, Bedfordshire. In October 1975 a GL version was added to the range, with improved trim and a centre console, plus large section tyres. Further changes took place in the following January. The range now consisted of the E, L, GL and GLS. Shortly afterwards the two- and four-door versions were announced and from September 1976 the estate car was in production, available only in 'L' trim specifications. Some very interesting limited production versions of the Chevette were produced with rallying in mind. The 2300 engine was fitted with 16-valve twin cam heads for the HS of 1976–79, which could be purchased for £5,317. The car was first in the Mintex International Rally of 24–26 February 1978 and first in the Finland Snow Rally of 17–19 February 1978 with Pentti Airikkala of Finland driving. The HS would go from 0–60 mph in 8.5 seconds; slightly faster was the 150 bhp HSR, priced at £7,146. In all, the HS scored eleven rally wins in the period 1977–9; the HSR repeated this fine effort in the period 1980–3. The Vauxhall drivers were Pentti Airikkala, Jimmy McRae, Tony Pond and Russell Brookes. In 1977 a Holman Blackburn Magnum driven by Gerry Marshall and Pete Brock won its class and came second in the Spa twenty-four hour race. This was the best result in a continental race since 1913!

The HSR was a development of the HS with wider wheel arches, side skirts, wider wheel rims, a revised back axle location and a twin-plate clutch. It was noisy, very fast and in its day it could beat Ford's Escort – quite simply the best British rally car of its time, and a case of history repeating itself.

The HC type Viva, introduced on 10 July 1971, expanded into a wide range of models, with engine sizes from 1159 cc to 2279 cc. The Firenza and the Magnum were both variations on the HC type. These Vivas date from 1963 (HA), 1966 (HB) and 1971 (HC), and the photograph was taken on 14 June 1971 – for release on 20 July, when the millionth Viva was due to be built.

A prototype HC type Viva GLS 1800, which developed into the Magnum.

A 1974 Viva SL. Changes included wider wheels, matt black non-reflecting wiper blades and arms. The fog lights, wing mirrors and rear warning lamp were factory-approved accessories.

The HC Viva estate car had the fastback roof line of the larger FE types. Such designs limit the rear luggage area owing to the intrusion of the tailgate and roof.

A 1972 Firenza 1600 SL. The Firenza was Luton's answer to the Ford Capri. Opel's Manta was a better alternative.

The 1974 Magnum 2300 coupé had fancy alloy wheels, four circular headlights and protective rubber inserts in the side mouldings and bumpers.

The FE type Victor/Ventora/VX range came in a number of trim and engine variations. The floor pan was of Opel origin but the rest was British, apart from the 3.3-litre Chevrolet six-cylinder engine fitted to the Ventora and the German Cetrag five-speed gearbox fitted to the final VX4/90 of 1977–78.

The Ventora estate was stylish, but how many sales were lost to Ford and Volvo because of the smaller luggage area?

The best looking FE model is the Ventora. Early examples had the centre part of the grille sprayed silver. In 1974 this was changed to black. Also from 1974, all models in the FE range were fitted with radial tyres as standard. The Ventora of the 1970s makes a very practical classic car today.

The interior of a 1974 Victor 2300 SL. The seats were not as comfortable as they look. The gearchange was poor and the clutch and brake pedals were at different heights, all of which caused adverse comment in road tests at the time.

The final FE designs were modified Victors and VX4/90s of 1976–78. The range was renamed VX, consisting of VX 1800 and VX 2300. The revised VX4/90 did not arrive until 1977. This is the VX 2300.

The revised VX4/90 of 1977.

The limited edition VX 2300 of 1977.

The Chevette was the replacement for the HC Viva range. The design was international, based on an Opel floor pan but using Vauxhall engines for the British market. After the Chevette Vauxhall cars were rebadged Opels. The Chevette was very successful both as an everyday car and also in motor sport. Today there are a number of clubs for the Vauxhall enthusiast. In recent years interest has grown in old Vauxhalls. Whether your choice is a 30/98 or an A type, or perhaps an FE Ventora from more recent times, you will find that the best of yesterday's Vauxhalls make very enjoyable old cars when restored.

What might have been! To conclude this brief account of Vauxhall's long and fascinating history, here are three cars that never reached the showroom. Vauxhall's experimental two-seater, the XVR, was 'an exercise in specification and form to indicate possible future trends in the design of high-performance vehicles', to quote the press release. The integrally constructed body, with its low centre of gravity, excellent weight distribution and low drag factor, was ingeniously designed around a central load-bearing backbone. The centre section opened on a single pivot, in place of conventional doors, while the bonnet pivoted forward and the rear body section pivoted backwards to give access to the boot. XVR was 13 ft 4 in long and 5 ft 4½ in wide – but only 3 ft 4 in high. There were no fixed engine and transmission specifications, as this was not part of the design study.

Vauxhall's SRV, like the XVR, was never intended as a production car: it was purely a styling exercise. First appearing at the Earls Court Motor Show in 1970, the SRV was a full four-seater four-door car, designed to have a mid-mounted turbo-charged engine. The body was glassfibre reinforced with carbonfibre. Unusually, the front doors hinged on the windscreen posts while the rear doors opened in the reverse direction, being hinged on the rear quarter roof rails. The SRV was an imposing vehicle: 16 ft 8 in long, 6 ft 4½ in wide and 3 ft 5½ in high. Some novel touches were included to improve roadholding – with an aerofoil in the nose and electric levelling at the rear.

The SRV instrument panel was mounted in the driver's door, and swung outward when the door was opened, to ease access. Although the instruments were mock-ups only, they included (as well as a conventional speedometer and revcounter) a manometer, to collate air pressure readings from all over the car's surface; a fuel distribution gauge, to show the allocation of fuel between various tanks; and no fewer than three instruments relating to the turbocharger – boost gauge, tachometer and exhaust gas temperature.

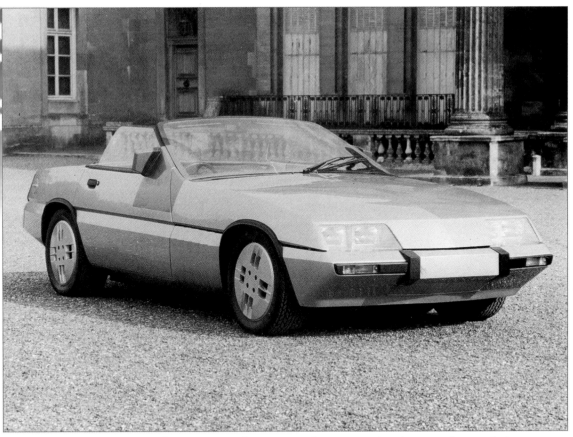

Released unexpectedly at the NEC Motor Show in 1978, the Equus was based on a Panther Lima's chassis frame and shared with it the highly regarded 2.3-litre Vauxhall engine. As the press release said: 'Although there are no production plans for the car at present, Vauxhall looks forward with very great interest to the public reaction the showing of the concept will bring.' The striking styling, especially when seen in silver with dark blue leather seats and red carpet, ensured an enthusiastic reception at the Motor Show – but sadly the car never entered production.

# ACKNOWLEDGEMENTS

The author would like to thank the following people, all of whom helped with the production of this book: the late Geoffrey King, and his widow Rita; the late Maurice Platt; Tony Burnip and Marian Hoenes of Vauxhall Motors; Marie Tische, Annie Collet and Mike Sandy of the National Motor Museum, Beaulieu; John Mullen, Nigel Starkey and Tony Newlove of the Vauxhall Owners Club; David Asplin; Jan Jensen; Laurie Seymour; Nic Portway; Bernard Ridgeley and Ray Cooper of Vauxhall Motors Heritage Collection.

The information in this book is true, and complete to the best of the author's knowledge. All recommendations are made without any guarantee on the part of the author or publisher, who also disclaim any liability incurred in connection with the use of this data or specific details.

# BRITAIN IN OLD PHOTOGRAPHS

To order any of these titles please telephone our distributor, Littlehampton Book Services on 01903 721596
For a catalogue of these and our other titles please ring Regina Schinner on 01453 731114